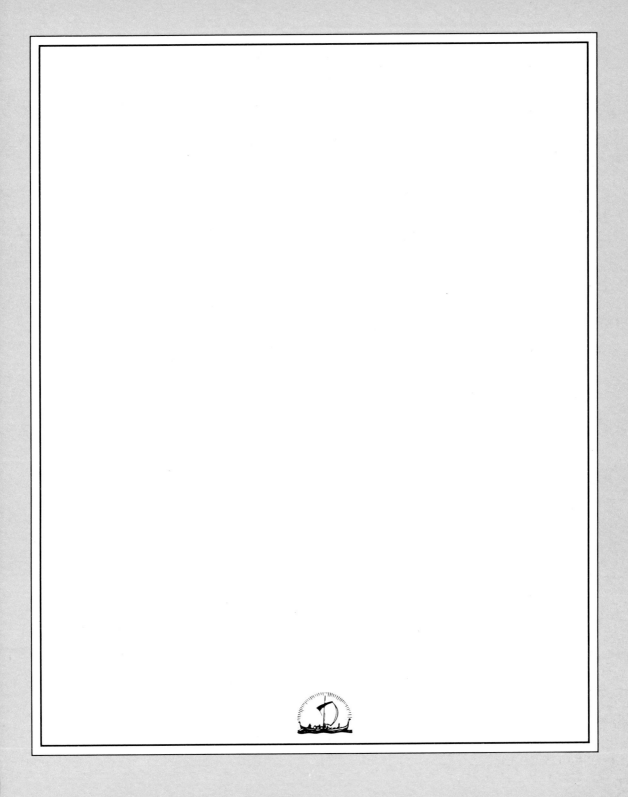

PHILIP ALLISON

LIFE IN THE
WHITE MAN'S GRAVE

A PICTORIAL RECORD OF THE BRITISH
IN WEST AFRICA

VIKING

VIKING

Penguin Books Ltd, 27 Wrights Lane, London w8 5tz (Publishing and Editorial)
and Harmondsworth, Middlesex, England (Distribution and Warehouse)
Viking Penguin Inc., 40 West 23rd Street, New York, New York 10010, USA
Penguin Books Australia Ltd, Ringwood, Victoria, Australia
Penguin Books Canada Ltd, 2801 John Street, Markham, Ontario, Canada l3r 1b4
Penguin Books (NZ) Ltd, 182–190 Wairau Road, Auckland 10, New Zealand

First published 1988

Copyright © Philip Allison, 1988

Map by Reginald Piggott

Typeset in 11/13 Monophoto Ehrhardt Semi-Bold
Printed and bound in Great Britain by
Butler & Tanner Ltd, Frome and London
Designed by Judith Gordon

British Library Cataloguing in Publication Data

Allison, Philip
Life in the white man's grave: a pictorial
record of the British in West Africa.
1. Africa, West – Colonization   2. Africa,
West – History   3. Great Britain – History
– 19th century   4. Great Britain –
History – 20th century
I. Title
996   DT476.2

ISBN 0–670–81020–7

(Frontispiece) In the bush: Mrs Powis, wife of a gold prospector,
trying to make herself at home in camp (see the caption to page 139).

CONTENTS

Contents

Acknowledgements

I am very grateful to a number of kind friends who responded to my appeal for photographs of West Africa, and especially to those who have allowed me to publish some of them in this book:

Michael Atkinson, 130, 135; Sir Gawain Bell, 114, 126, 136, 138; Guy Betts, 94, 103; Michael Counsell, 137; Dr Peter Davies, 17–19; Mrs June Hopkins, 129; Anthony Kirk-Greene, 70–71; Eric Lanning, 99, 106; Lady Marshall, 107, 131; Mrs Margaret Othick, 89; F. C. Powis, 53, 98, 101, 120; Frank Willett, 75.

The following photographs appear by courtesy of: Foreign and Commonwealth Office Library, 15–16, 31, 35–6, 40–42, 48–51, 54, 57–63, 72; House of Fraser, 95; Kirkwall Public Library, 11; Museum of Mankind, 2, 33, 37, 52, 55, 97; *Nigerian Field*, 64–5, 68, 100; private collection, 78, 83, 123–4; John Savory (photographs by the late H. J. Duckworth), 22–4, 73, 84, 86–7, 90–93, 105, 108–13, 115–16, 119, 122, 127–8; Mary Slessor Centre, Dundee, 14; United Africa Co., 21, 26, 45, 66–7, 74, 85, 102, 134.

Acknowledgements are made for the following to: BBC Hulton Picture Library, 7; Bodleian Library (Rhodes House), 39, 76–7, 80–82; Central Press Photos Ltd, 140; Church Missionary Society, 12–13; collection of the author, 25, 104; Liverpool Public Libraries, 20, 88; National Army Museum, 27, 32, 69; *Nigeria Magazine*, 117–18; *Optima*, 136; Lord Radnor, 1; Royal Commonwealth Society, 9, 43–4, 46–7; Royal Geographical Society, 79; West Africa Publications, 3, 34, 56, 125, 132; *West Africa Review*, 139.

It has not been possible to identify most of the early photographers. However, the photographs for plates 57–9 were taken by Dr J. W. Rowland, Colonial Surgeon, and for plates 21, 64–5, 68 and 74 by J. A. Green of the Photo House, Bonny.

Maps by Reginald Piggott.

Chronology by Dr S. M. Martin.

CHRONOLOGY

1444	Arrival of the Portuguese at the mouth of the Senegal River
1482	Establishment of the fort of Elmina (Gold Coast)
1661	Establishment of the British Company of Royal Adventurers (Royal Africa Company from 1672)
1763	British acquisition of French settlements on the Gambia River after the Seven Years War
1772	Abolition of slavery under English law by the Mansfield Judgment
1795–1805	Journeys of the Scottish explorer Dr Mungo Park along the Gambia and upper Niger rivers; he was drowned at Bussa in 1806
1804–8	Fulani led jihad (Muslim holy war) in Hausaland; foundation of Sokoto Caliphate (later part of Northern Nigeria)
1807	Abolition of the Atlantic slave trade by Britain; establishment of the Anti-Slavery Squadron at Freetown (Sierra Leone), declared a crown colony, 1808
1824	Death of Sir Charles M'Carthy, Governor of Sierra Leone and the Gold Coast settlements, in battle against the Ashanti
1827–9	Journey of the French explorer René Caillié along the cola trade routes to Timbuktu and across the Sahara to Tangier
1835	Under pressure from the Fulani, abandonment of Old Oyo (later in Western Nigeria) by its monarch, the Alafin
1850–55	Journeys of the German explorer, Heinrich Barth, across the Sahara from Tripoli to Bornu, the Sokoto Caliphate, and Timbuktu
1854	Successful steamer voyage up the lower Niger River by Dr William Baikie, financed by Liverpool merchant Macgregor Laird and pioneering the use of quinine to prevent malaria, following voyages led by the Lander brothers in 1830 and 1832, and organized by the British Government in 1841–2, which had very heavy mortality
1861	Annexation of Lagos by Britain
1873–4	Renewed British war with Ashanti; declaration of a crown colony in the southern Gold Coast
1885	Conference of Berlin: formal partition of Africa

1886	Grant of a royal charter to Sir George Goldie's Royal Niger Company
1891	Establishment of the Oil Rivers Protectorate, renamed the Niger Coast Protectorate in 1893; began extending its relations with the hinterland, 1894, through three journeys by Roger Casement (also a well-known Irish nationalist)
1891	British declaration of a protectorate over Ashanti, followed by deposition of leading chiefs in 1896 and insurrection, suppressed 1900
1896	British declaration of a protectorate over hinterland of Sierra Leone, followed by the Hut Tax War of 1898
1900	Establishment of the Protectorates of Northern and Southern Nigeria, including territory previously administered during the 1890s by the Royal Niger Company and the Niger Coast Protectorate. Gradual occupation was achieved after operations against the Benin (1897), Aro Chukwu (1902) and the Fulani emirates (1903)
1906	Colony of Lagos amalgamated with Protectorate of Southern Nigeria
1907–15	Debate over whether to grant plantation concessions to the British firm Lever Bros. in West Africa; final decision to leave land in African hands, in communal ownership
1914	Amalgamation of the Protectorates of Northern and Southern Nigeria
1929	Formation of the United Africa Company, which then dominated Southern Nigeria's export trade
1929–30	Women's Riots against taxation and falling export prices in Eastern Nigeria
1940–42	French West Africa under the Vichy régime; then switched to support de Gaulle
1941–5	South-East Asia under Japanese occupation; West African rubber and other exports vital to the Allies
1957	Independence of the Gold Coast (Ghana)
1958	Independence of Guinea
1960	Independence of Nigeria and the remaining French West African territories
1961	Independence of Sierra Leone
1965	Independence of the Gambia

FOREWORD

The main aim of an author's foreword is, I suppose, to disarm the critics by getting in first with criticism of his own work. This is a book of pictures which records incidents and personalities from a brief period of colonial history that may soon be forgotten. Some may say: 'The sooner the better.' But the facts of history are always worth preserving and should never be obliterated. The only valid criticism of the pictures that I can see is that there are not enough of them. There must be many relevant illustrations which I have not traced and there are many which the limitations of the book prevent me from including.

The text consists of a brief historical sketch, to provide a link between the episodes and characters illustrated, and a few pages of personal reminiscence which may help to illuminate the history.

A very amateur historian who attempts to give an account of five centuries of history in 20,000 words inevitably lays himself open to criticism on general grounds and particularly, perhaps, for spreading unevenly what is bound to be a superficial account. I don't think that Nigeria receives undue attention in text and pictures, considering that she occupied about 75 per cent of the land area of old British West Africa and accommodated a rather higher proportion of the total population. In addition, I spent thirty years of my working life in Nigeria.

If Lugard takes up too much of a brief narrative, it is because his life story is particularly relevant to this period in colonial history; he himself documented it so fully and Margery Perham made it so accessible and readable. If there is too much of Mungo Park and not enough of Barth and some others, it is because Park is my favourite explorer.

It is not only the facts of history that have been abridged, of course. Some who read this book may feel that the enormities of the slave trade, the horrors of colonial wars and the looting of Kumasi and Benin have been passed over with little more than a bare mention and no attempt at either justification or excuse. On the other hand, some will consider that the achievements of the British in West Africa have been inadequately recognized. Again I must plead that this is a picture book, and hope that you will look at the pictures and reach your own conclusions.

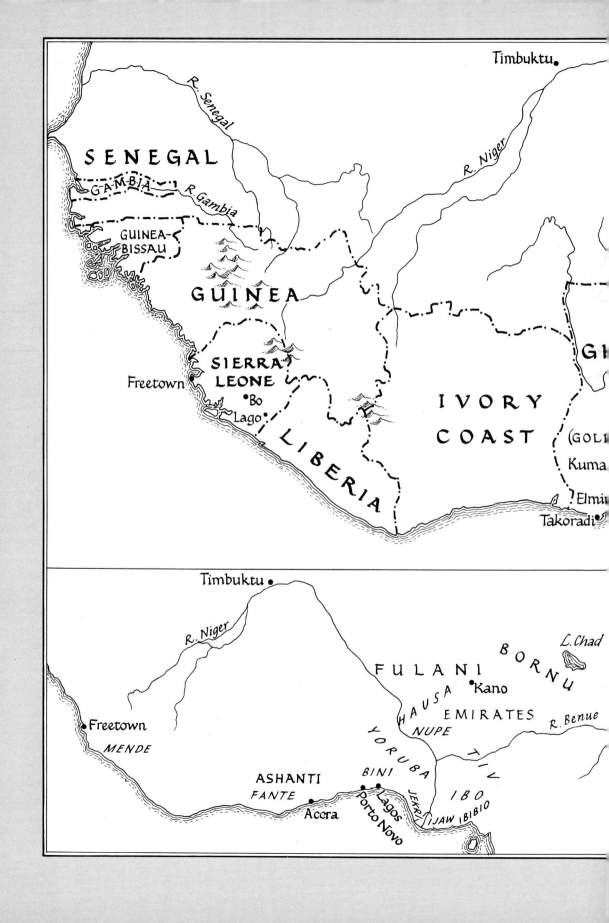

L. Chad

Sokoto

Katsina

Kano
Maiduguri

N I G E R I A

Kontagora

BENIN (DAHOMEY)
Bussa
Minna

TOGO
Jebba
Bida

Ilorin
Lokoja

NA
Iseyin
Oyo
R. Benue

Ibadan

(OAST)
Abeokuta
Ondo
Ubiaja

R. Volta
IjebuOde
Okitipupa
Enugu

Lagos
Benin City
Onitsha
Cross R.

Badagri
Sapele

Porto Novo
Siluko R.
Degema
Pt. Harcourt

Accra
Forcados
Calabar

pe Coast
Abonema
Douala

Niger Delta
Bonny

Bight of Benin
CAMEROON

Fernando Po

Equator

G U L F   O F   G U I N E A

0   500 miles

0   500   1000km

WEST AFRICA. THE INSET SHOWS PEOPLES AND PRE-COLONIAL
STATES

I

LIFE IN THE WHITE MAN'S GRAVE

Beware and take care of the Bight of Benin
There's one comes out for forty goes in.

During the first centuries of European contact with West Africa, this sinister estimate of mortality was no exaggeration. In the coastal creeks and estuaries where the first voyagers sheltered from the Atlantic rollers, they could see the white mist curling up off the dark, still waters as the sun rose, and smell the warm, damp, rotten-sweet land breeze. And they thought it was the very air they breathed – the bad air, the malaria – that brought on the fever and the sweats and the shakes that were the beginning of the end for many.

This frightful death rate continued for five hundred years before its cause was traced to an insect bite. It was the mosquito, the carrier of the malarial parasite, that delayed penetration and prevented European settlement of West Africa. In recognition of the part played by this powerful ally against colonization, one of the early Nigerian political parties adopted the mosquito as its electioneering emblem.

This book presents a pictorial record of the British in West Africa. Until the end of the nineteenth century this connection was confined to a few small trading settlements on the coast, and the official association between Britain and the largest and richest of her possessions lasted only sixty years: many Nigerians lived to see the white man come and go.

Africa was the scene of the last fling of the British imperial adventure, and much of that brief incident was recorded in photographs. We have portraits of the last of the explorers who sometimes became the first administrators, as did Dr Baikie and Captain Glover. The pre-photographic period was sparsely illustrated with engravings and prints, and the earliest visitors of all were depicted in brass by their African hosts.

DISCOVERY

The first European voyagers down the West Coast were the Portuguese of the fifteenth century. They were merchants, exploring a sea route to India and the spice trade, and ready to pick up any profitable cargoes on the way. They were missionaries intent on spreading Christianity, as they did in the Congo and, briefly, in Benin. They were political agents, hoping to contact allies on the flank of the Muslim states that threatened Portugal from Spain and North Africa and blocked the overland trade routes through the Levant to India. The main items of this trade were recorded in the names given to the various sections of the coast to the east of Cape Palmas: Ivory Coast, Gold Coast and Slave Coast. Of these, the name *Côte d'Ivoire* alone has survived freedom from colonial rule.

In addition to providing a valuable commodity, the elephant was considered to have an exemplary moral character. According to Richard Hakluyt: 'they are of quicke sense and sharpness of wit ... insomuch that they learne to do honor to a king'; 'they use none adulterie'; 'if they happen to meete with a man in the wildernesse, being out of the way, gently they wil go before him, & bring him into the plaine way'; and 'They have continual warre against Dragons, which desire their blood because it is very cold'.[1]

The elephants of West Africa survived the attacks of the dragons but eventually suffered near extinction at the hands of the elephant hunters and ivory traders. Ivory was normally exported in the form of tusks, but a few specimens of carved ivory found their way into Europe at this time. These are in the form of ornate cups, bowls and trumpets carved by African artists, probably from the Sierra Leone and Yoruba areas. They depict African figures, fantastic beasts and bearded Europeans wearing sixteenth-century dress and equipment, and appear to have been made to the order of European traders who brought them home as souvenirs, where they have survived in early collections of curios.

GOLD AND SLAVES

Before the establishment of the transatlantic colonies, which provided the market for African slaves, the Portuguese had already tapped the sources of the gold that had hitherto reached Europe by way of the Sahara trade routes and North Africa, and by the end of the fifteenth century they had established themselves in a strong, stone-built fort at Elmina on the Gold Coast. The African traders accepted slaves as well as European goods in exchange for gold and ivory, and a coastwise import in slaves, from the Niger Delta and elsewhere, predated the Atlantic export trade. For nearly a hundred years the Portuguese monopolized this valuable gold trade, but by the end of the seventeenth century they had been ousted by the Dutch, English and Danes, who established some thirty trading forts along the coast which continually changed hands as a result of European wars, local deals and skirmishes.

As European colonization of the West Indies and the Americas developed, the slave trade grew and flourished. For more than two hundred years the contacts of the white man with Africa were overshadowed and vitiated by the horrors of the trade in black men. When, in 1833, the status of slavery was finally abolished in all British possessions, William Wilberforce wrote: 'That such a system should so long have been suffered to exist in any part of the British Empire will appear to our posterity almost incredible.'[2]

The appalling callousness with which the trade was conducted is horribly illustrated by the notorious case of the slave ship *Zong*, whose captain threw overboard more than a hundred sick slaves in order to qualify for compensation under a clause in his insurance policy. The incident is dramatically recorded in a painting by Turner.

Trading posts and trade monopolies were bandied about between the nations of Europe by treaty and sale. As a result of Marlborough's victories, England won the *asiento*: a monopoly contract for supplying slaves to the Spanish possessions in America. And, as part of the spoils of the Seven Years War, a strip of land along the Gambia River became Britain's first African colony.

The African suppliers, and certainly the African cargoes which they supplied, were little concerned whether the shippers were English, Dutch or French. The goods exchanged for slaves consisted of European manufactures such as cloth, spirits and hardware, but also included guns and powder which were used by the primary producers in slave-catching wars up-country. In an attempt to deal directly with the shippers, the slave catchers sometimes turned their guns on the coastal middlemen and even on the European shippers themselves when they came to the defence of their trading partners.

Last Days of the Slave Trade

The sheltered anchorages among the creeks and islands of the coast of Sierra Leone had long been a favourite haunt of slavers and pirates. But towards the end of the eighteenth century these became the scene of an early experiment in emancipation. A judgment reluctantly given by Lord Chief Justice Mansfield, in 1772, resulted in the freeing of 15,000 slaves then resident in Britain. Many of these exchanged the status of slave for that of pauper. In an attempt to solve the problem of the 'black poor', four hundred unemployed ex-slaves and sixty white prostitutes were callously shipped out to Sierra Leone and settled on twenty square miles of land bought from a local chief.

After such a start, it is hardly surprising that the settlement did not flourish; but it did survive, at first under the control of the Sierra Leone Trading Company and later, after the slave trade had been declared an illegal occupation for British subjects, as a crown colony.

From being the most successful participators in the trade, the British now became the most effective force for its suppression. Freetown, Sierra Leone, was established as a base of operations for the Anti-Slavery Squadron of the Royal Navy and a settlement for the accommodation of the human cargoes freed from the captured slave ships. Denmark had indeed declared the trade to be illegal four years previously, and now the British Government, by a mixture of bribery and coercion, persuaded the other nations to legislate against it also. This gave a legal sanction to operations by the British Navy against non-British participators in the trade. Long after the trade had been declared illegal, the institution of slavery continued to operate in the United States, Brazil and elsewhere.

The drive for abolition arose from the liberal and humanitarian convictions that inspired the French Revolution, though the decree of emancipation passed by the revolutionary government was revoked by Napoleon. At the same time it may have occurred to the hard-headed plantation owners of the Americas that the employment of free labour, which could be laid off and taken on again as required, might be a better proposition than slave labour which not only failed to reproduce itself, but actively revolted against the authority of its masters. Indeed, in Haiti a slave revolt achieved complete independence from France before the end of the eighteenth century.

THE EXPLORERS

This was an age of scientific inquiry. The early European voyagers had been activated by economic, religious and political motives. The nineteenth-century African explorers accepted incredible privations and dangers, ostensibly at least, in pursuit of geographical knowledge, though they must have been strongly moved by that powerful but imponderable force, the spirit of adventure. They were financed – though far from generously – by the Association for Promoting the Discovery of the Interior Parts of Africa, whose members (in 1788) issued this statement of their aims:

That as no species of information is more ardently desired or more generally useful, than that which improves the science of Geography; and as the vast Continent of Africa, notwithstanding the efforts of the Ancients, and the wishes of the Moderns, is still in a great measure unexplored, the members of this club do form themselves into an Association for Promoting the Discovery of the Inland Parts of that Quarter of the World.[3]

So, from their cosy London clubroom at the St Alban's Tavern, the members of the Association sent out a succession of brave young men to discover the inland parts of Africa, the majority of whom laid their bones there.

One of the most puzzling questions of African geography concerned the course of the Niger. The last traveller to have recorded a visit to the banks of this great river was the sixteenth-century Arab traveller known as Leo Africanus. He had bedevilled African geography for two hundred years by stating that, in the neighbourhood of Timbuktu, the Niger flowed from east to west. If this was true, it was presumed to reach the sea through the mouth of either the Senegal or the Gambia. If, on the other hand, Leo was mistaken, it might debouch through the Congo or even flow clean across Africa to become a tributary of the Nile. The fact that the Niger emerged unobtrusively through the creeks of a great delta was only to be revealed after another forty years had passed and many lives had been lost in the search.

The first to be able to correct this strange mistake was the young Scots doctor Mungo Park. During the last years of the century, Park set off from a trading post up the Gambia River, accompanied by two African servants, on an ill-equipped expedition which lasted three years. When only a week's journey short of the river, he was captured by a party of Moorish slavers who viewed Park with suspicion and intense curiosity. The brass buttons on his European clothes were objects of great interest and he was soon relieved of most of them. On one occasion he was visited by a party of Moorish women who (he records) wished 'to ascertain, by actual inspection, whether the rite of circumcision extended to Nazarenes, as well as to followers of Mahomet'. He offered to 'give ocular demonstration ... if all of them would retire except the young lady to whom I pointed [selecting the youngest and handsomest]

... she did not avail herself of the privilege ... but the ladies enjoyed the jest'.[4] Park's sense of humour supported him through the most depressing, frustrating and dangerous circumstances.

He escaped from the Moors and eventually, 'at the moderate price of a button' (one of the few remaining), he was directed to the object of his quest: 'the majestic Niger, glittering in the morning sun, broad as the Thames at Westminster and flowing slowly to the Eastward'. Once again Park was stripped of all his possessions, except his papers, and he literally begged his way back to the Gambia on foot.

Eight years later he was back in Africa, in charge of a better-equipped expedition. By the time he reached the river all but four out of his forty European companions had died. This much reduced party embarked on a suitably converted canoe. Once on board and headed downstream, Park seems to have been determined that nothing should stop him reaching the sea and he appears to have shot his way through any real or fancied opposition. When still some 700 miles from the sea, his boat foundered in the rapids below Bussa and, perhaps under attack from the bank, Park and all the crew were drowned except for one slave boy. The Emirs of Bussa have always maintained that Park and his crew were drowned in the rapids in spite of friendly warnings and attempts to save them.

The successful lone traveller who wins his way through by friendly persuasion, but who brings disaster on himself and his companions when he finds himself in the position to resort to force, appears several times in the history of African exploration. The happy traveller Richard Lander was another example of this unhappy transformation. He first visited Africa as the servant of the explorer Captain Hugh Clapperton, who died in Sokoto in 1826. Lander made his way back to the coast and home to England. Early in 1830, accompanied by his brother John, he returned to land at Badagri, on the coast west of Lagos. The brothers trekked up overland to Bussa and followed the river downstream. They finished the journey in the hands of Ibo raiders who sold them to an Ijaw chief. They were finally rescued by the captain of a Liverpool brig who was loading palm oil in the delta.

MERCHANT VENTURERS

The most promising successor to the slave trade was the trade in palm oil. The creeks of the Niger Delta tapped an extensive oil-producing area, and the discovery that these creeks formed a navigable waterway to the interior of the continent had obvious commercial possibilities.

An enterprising Liverpool merchant, Macgregor Laird, lost no time in fitting out a trading expedition. Twenty months after his rescue, Richard Lander joined Laird, and they sailed in one of the iron-hulled paddle steamers that the merchant had built especially for the journey.

Lander had survived two ill-equipped expeditions: the armaments provided for him and his brother had consisted of 'one fowling piece and one pistol each'. But Laird's lavish supplies and equipment tempted the piratically inclined Ijaws of the Niger Delta to attack one of the supply canoes, and Lander received gunshot wounds from which he died. Only nine of the forty-eight Europeans survived the expedition, with most members dying of malaria and dysentery. Subsequent expeditions showed similar frightful records of European mortality, which discouraged Niger explorations for the next twenty years.

The Frenchman René Caillié had already visited Timbuktu, and Dr Heinrich Barth (a German employed by the British Government) spent five years in Bornu, Kano and other major Sudanese centres that flourished on the caravan trade with North Africa. These travellers survived many difficulties and dangers, but the climate of the Sudan and its attendant diseases were less hazardous to Europeans than those of the coastal creeks and forests, where the Royal Navy's Anti-Slavery Squadron soon earned the title of the 'Coffin Squadron'.

The great medical breakthrough came in 1854 when the iron-screw steamer *Pleiad* remained in the Niger for four months with a crew of fifty-four Africans and twelve Europeans, without loss of life, thanks to the regular use of quinine. Although the full life-cycle of the mosquito-borne parasite was not discovered until the last years of the century, and the cautionary tale of the 'white man's grave' persisted, it was five grains of quinine a day that stood between the Europeans and a West African grave until various marginally more effective substitutes were developed during the Second World War.

The commander of the *Pleiad* was Dr William Baikie, a young naval surgeon from Orkney. The remarkable health record of this voyage encouraged Macgregor Laird to accept a government contract to send an annual trading vessel up the Niger. The first of these, the *Dayspring*, was again commanded by Baikie. His second in command was Lieutenant John Glover, who became one of the early governors of Lagos. The Government had hopes that the opportunities for legitimate trade offered by Laird's contract ship and the moral force exerted by the missionaries who accompanied the expedition would combine to bring an end to the slave trade. Though Laird, whose previous ventures had suffered from attacks by the delta tribes, had been heard to define 'moral force' as a 'thirty-two pounder with an English sailor standing behind it'.

Baikie established a base at Lokoja, at the Niger–Benue confluence, with the aim of opening up trade with the Muslim emirates to the north. But Laird's steamers arrived irregularly, due to the hostility of the delta tribes and seasonal low water in the Niger; and when his trade goods ran out, Baikie had to rely on the charity of the slave-raiding Emir of Nupe. He established a Freed Slaves' Home, translated the Bible into Hausa and raised a half-caste family. His attitude to life at the confluence fluctuated inconveniently. When the steamer failed to appear, Baikie wrote to the Foreign Office, begging to be relieved; but by the time the relief boat arrived, he felt that his work was making good progress and refused to desert his post. When, after seven years at the confluence, he did at last set out for home, Baikie did not survive the voyage and was buried at Sierra Leone.

Reluctant Imperialists

In spite of the efforts of the British Navy, the export of slaves continued, especially from Lagos where, in 1851, a naval assault was mounted with the aim of installing a chief who was willing to abolish the trade. A British consul was posted and, ten years later, Lagos was annexed outright. At about the same time an Ashanti army invaded the British 'protected' territories of the Gold Coast virtually unopposed. British prestige on the coast was at its lowest and, in spite of the recent acquisition of Lagos, a House of Commons Committee of 1865 advised that:

all further extensions of territory or assumption of Government (in West Africa) ... would be inexpedient and that the object of policy should be to encourage in the natives the exercise of those qualities which may render it possible for us more and more to transfer to them the administration of all the governments, with a view to our ultimate withdrawal from all, except, probably, Sierra Leone.[5]

If Colonial Office policies were subject to change, so too were the attitudes of the 'men on the spot'. The young Lieutenant Glover described the voyage of the *Dayspring* as 'a new Crusade against the Muslim ... only we will hope a bloodless one'.[6] Baikie, the commander of the expedition, considered, more prosaically, that the most beneficial achievement of his previous voyage was to have opened up 'a most important outlet for home manufactures, as the unclad millions of Central Africa must absorb thousands of cargoes of soft goods, eagerly bartering their raw cotton, their vegetable oils and ivory for our calico cloths'.[7]

To convert the heathen or profitably to clothe him: which should be the aim of the colonial power? Cecil Rhodes had the answer a few years later: 'Philanthropy is all very well but philanthropy plus three per cent is a good deal better.'

The 'bloodless crusader' of the *Dayspring* became the forceful Governor of Lagos: 'too ready to enlarge his territory and draw the sword', in the opinion of the Colonial Secretary. Glover had proudly reported that he had raised the flag in the nearby town of Ikpokia only to be brusquely ordered to go and take it down again.

That the policy of scuttle to get out could so soon be converted to one of scramble to get into Africa seems to have been due to several factors. At this period there were six changes of Colonial Secretary in the space of ten years and the resulting vacillations of government policy were sometimes overridden by zealous men on the spot, like Glover, or, perhaps more often, directed by the prodding and lobbying of commercial interests at home.

European rivalries provided an added stimulus. The French Government, subject to similar commercial pressures, saw a prospect of compensating for the defeat of 1870, while the newly unified German state, alarmed at being left behind in the race, hastily slipped in between the French and British to occupy Togo and Cameroon. In an attempt to control and regularize this confused and potentially dangerous situation, in 1885 France and Germany set up the Berlin Conference, at which it was decided that the various, ill-defined spheres of influence claimed by the European powers should be confirmed by effective occupation. Britain could claim to have established official occupation of the coast of Sierra Leone, the Gold Coast and the Niger coast from Lagos to the Cross River, but any claim to the vast area of the Lower Niger and Benue Basin rested on treaties made between African chiefs and a commercial trading company.

TRADE AND THE FLAG

George Goldie, an ex-Army officer with financial interests in one of the Niger trading firms, persuaded all the other British companies to amalgamate and finally, on the eve of the Berlin Conference, bought out two remaining French companies and could claim unquestioned

British influence in the area. A year later the company was granted a royal charter, under the name of the Royal Niger Company, and, until 1900, exercised what was virtually a trade monopoly of the Lower Niger and Benue, and policed and administered as much of the area as could be reached from the main waterways.

Between the British advance from the south and the French from Senegal and Algeria, the wide plains of the Sudan were still dominated by several powerful figures who divided this vast area between them, each exacting tribute in the form of slaves, from his own sphere of influence. To the west, Samory the Mandigo controlled the hinterland from Sierra Leone to the Gold Coast. To the east, Rabeh, an invader from the Sudan, occupied the Lake Chad area. Both were finally dealt with by the advancing French, leaving the Fulani emirs at the centre to be absorbed into the British Protectorate of Northern Nigeria, which took over from the Royal Niger Company at the beginning of the century, with Sir Frederick Lugard as High Commissioner.

Lugard's career conforms closely to the popular idea of the life of the African empire builder, and reads like an adventure story written for the *Boy's Own Paper* at the turn of the century. He saw service in India, the Sudan and Burma as an Army officer. An unhappy love-affair affected this apparently unemotional young man so severely that he was granted a prolonged sick leave. He drifted down the coast of East Africa and considered shooting elephants for their ivory, but ended up organizing a campaign against Arab slavers on behalf of a Christian mission which ran a trading company on Lake Nyasa. Subsequently, in the employment of the Imperial East African Company and in competition with the Germans, he laid the foundations of British rule in Uganda.

After an eventful four years in East Africa, he took service with Goldie's Royal Niger Company and beat the French in a close-run treaty-making dash to the present western borders of Nigeria. Two years later he returned with a Colonial Office appointment to raise an official body of troops to defend these same boundaries against the French.

Chamberlain, at the Colonial Office, had already realized that the time had come for the Government to buy out the company and assume full administrative responsibility for the Niger country. When the proposal came before Parliament, however, little enthusiasm was shown for this new acquisition. In the course of the debate, John Dillon, an Irish Member, expressed the doubts of the Liberal opposition: 'I refuse to recognize as a great gift to this country an addition of 35 millions of unknown people ... and nobody can forecast the extent of evil which may result from this great accession to the territory of the British Empire.'[8] As an Irish Republican, Dillon's attitude to colonialism differed from that of most Members present and the take-over was approved by a majority of one hundred.

But were Dillon's apprehensions justified? Perhaps this question can best be disposed of by asking another: what was the alternative? At this period of world history no part of Africa could hope to escape European domination, and those West Africans whose countries found themselves under British rule at this time might concede, when they consider some of the alternatives, that their fate could have been worse.

Whether or not the possession of African colonies was eventually of much direct economic advantage to the possessor powers now seems doubtful, but one lasting benefit to Britain from her imperial adventures is that some of the finest literature from the Third World is now being written in the English language.

THE FLAG TO THE FORE

Virtually the only contact with Africa made by Europeans during the centuries of the long pre-colonial period was through their trading partners: such coastal peoples as the Fante of the Gold Coast and the Ijaws and Jekri of the Niger Delta. The well-disciplined Ashanti armies from the forests of the interior had made their presence felt down at the coast by the beginning of the nineteenth century, but, as we shall see, the Ashanti remained independent of British rule until 1901, when Lugard was first making contact with the Fulani emirs of Northern Nigeria.

The people of the western Sudan, to the north of the forest belt, had probably adopted Islam at some time during the thirteenth century. Such city states as Kano and Sokoto had grown rich on trade across the desert to North Africa, mainly in staples such as gold, slaves and ivory. The Hausa population of these large walled towns, as well as being traders and farmers, also engaged in the manufacture of textiles, metal work, leather work and other crafts. At the beginning of the nineteenth century the Hausa states were forcibly united by a war of religious revival led by the Fulani, a non-Negro people of mysterious origins.

The Royal Niger Company had concluded trade treaties with the Fulani emirs, whose wealth and power were based on slavery and the trade in slaves. The company declared the abolition of slavery within its territories, but was powerless to enforce such an abolition or to put a stop to slave raiding.

Lugard received hostile replies to his friendly approaches to the Sultan of Sokoto (the Fulani leader) and, when one of his political officers was murdered by a minor Fulani chief, he dispatched a small military force with the declared aim of arresting the murderer, who fled for protection to the Emir of Kano.

Lugard followed close behind the military operation, which was brief but bloody, and in little more than six weeks personally received the submission of the four most important emirates. Meanwhile, the ancient Kanuri state of Bornu, under attack by the French, surrendered to the British as the lesser of two evils. The ruling Fulani were still regarded as alien conquerors and commanded little support from the Hausa peasantry. Lugard, however, found that the existing system of Islamic law courts and tax collection through district heads could work with reasonable efficiency and equity under the supervision of his Residents. Northern Nigerian finances depended on subventions from a parsimonious home government and reimposition of emirate rule was above all an economical means of running the country.

To put an end to slave raiding was the first concern of the British administration, but to abolish at a stroke the ancient and universal institution of slavery itself would have caused social and economic chaos. It was decreed that, from 1 April 1901, all children were born free and the legal status of slavery was abolished, so that the master of a run-away slave had no legal redress.

In the space of little over two years Lugard established a degree of control which it had taken ten times as long to achieve in Southern Nigeria over an area less than half the size. Expansion from the various consular stations on the coast had been extremely cautious, to match the British Government's initial reluctance to extend its African possessions. By the end of the century, however, Chamberlain's expansionist colonial policy at home was complemented by Lugard's energy and enthusiasm in the field.

INDIRECT RULE

To the north of Lagos, the Fulani *jihad* had pressed southwards into the Yoruba country, which resulted in the break-up of the Oyo empire and a struggle for power between the various component Yoruba states. The Alafin of Oyo finally appealed to the Governor of Lagos for help in bringing these confused hostilities to an end. Thus the British came as peace-makers, and the exhausted combatants offered little opposition to the treaty-making tours of officers from the Lagos Government. By

the end of the century, British Residents and Travelling Commissioners
had been posted to ensure that the terms of the treaties were being
complied with. The limited conditions covered by such treaties are
illustrated in this directive issued by the Governor of Lagos in 1893:

> For the guidance of District Commissioners His Excellency the Governor
> desires to point out that upon the inclusion of native territories within the
> Protectorate of Lagos, certain conditions have invariably been laid down, which
> are briefly as follows:
>   1st That the practice of offering human sacrifice be abolished.
>   2nd That Her Majesty reserves to Herself the power of life and death.
>   Outside these conditions it has not been the intention of Her Majesty to
> interfere with native customs, jurisdiction or administration.[9]

Mindful of these instructions, Governor MacGregor, reporting on a tour
of the Yoruba country a few years later, recorded a conversation with
the Alafin of Oyo during which he wrote: 'I raised, quite frankly, the
question of eunuchs. It was explained to the Alafin that there was no
wish to interfere with his present domestic arrangements ...'[10] But a
nominal role for these important palace dignitaries was requested, just
for the record, and a list of twenty-one names was submitted.

In the same report MacGregor wrote: 'It is necessary that DOs
[District Officers] should understand that we can rule the country only
through the chiefs.' Lugard has often been seen as the originator of the
system of indirect rule in Africa, and it was he who exhaustively
recorded the political situation as he found it operating in the emirates
and codified his adaptation of it in his political memoranda. But this
basic idea, simply expressed by MacGregor, occurred to many British
administrators in Africa and was applied, with varying success, in a
variety of situations.

Among the Akan people of the Gold Coast colony, the respect shown
by the British for native law and custom prevented the traditional chiefs
from acting as satisfactory links in the chain of authority. Here, the
members of the community qualified to appoint the chief were also
qualified to depose him, which they quickly did whenever he attempted
to introduce any unpopular administrative measure, such as the imposition of tax.

When Lugard met for the first time the powerful Yoruba obas, he
wrote: 'the Alafin [of Oyo] is anxious to accept the same status as the
paramount Emirs of the North ...'.[11] The obas, whose traditional powers
were by no means as absolute as Lugard assumed, never had it so good

as in the early years of British administration, but when an attempt was made to introduce through them the alien system of direct taxation, there was riot and bloodshed at Oyo and Abeokuta. Even the semi-divine powers of the Oba of Benin were limited by the authority of a group of chiefs who constituted a form of official opposition.

Among the Ijaws of the delta, whose way of life had for centuries been geared to trade with Europeans, a peculiar system known as 'house rule' was recognized for a time. Here authority was found to be in the hands of trading chiefs whose wealth and power depended on their ability to man a fleet of canoes which were used for the purposes of trade or war. The powers allowed to such a head over the members of his house, many of whom were slaves, amounted to the recognition of slave status until the House Rule Proclamation was repealed in 1914.

Over much of the country to the east of the Niger and in the non-Muslim north, however, the family head often appeared to constitute the highest accepted authority and where some form of superior spiritual power existed, it was too nebulous to be administratively useful. Such communities, where they appeared in West Africa, presented the British administration with problems not so easily understood as those posed by the Muslim autocracies, with their echoes of the European feudal system. Once the power of the Fulani emirs had been broken, the Hausa peasantry bowed, often gratefully, to the rule of the conqueror. In the south-east, resistance to the occupation often had to be overcome village by village and, once occupied, the administration of the country was complicated by the traditional right claimed by every family head to be heard in the councils of the clan.

ONE NIGERIA

After five years' absence as Governor of Hong Kong, Lugard returned in 1912 to prepare for the amalgamation of Northern and Southern Nigeria. The creation of the Colony and Protectorate of Nigeria was completed on 1 January 1914. Eight months later, these internal problems were further complicated by the necessity to launch a military campaign against the Germans in adjacent Cameroon.

His six years among the emirs of Northern Nigeria had prepared him for the degree of authority exercised by the obas of the south-west. And he was quite willing to prescribe for the very different communities he now met to the east of the Niger, though the prescriptions, as we shall see, ultimately resulted in the tragedy of the Women's Riots. But he never came to terms with the élites of Lagos.

As in other coastal towns in West Africa, there existed in Lagos a small but influential cosmopolitan element who had adopted the religion and life-style of the colonial power. They considered that the democratic ideals professed by the British should lead to the adoption of more representative forms of government in which their education fitted them to participate, and viewed with suspicion the proposals to confirm the autocratic rule of the emirs and obas. Several English-language newspapers gave voice to the political aspirations of these élites. As early as 1863, the Lagos *Anglo African* stated its policy: 'not to serve any party, but in all questions to advocate the side of right – right, not in the estimation of this man or that, but in the estimation of the editor; and hence we shall never consult anyone as to what we shall say or what we shall forbear to say'.[12]

A new Governor-General with his emirate background was obviously a challenge to the aggressively free Lagos press. As Lugard wrote to his wife: 'The Colonial Office and the Faddists would never tolerate any infringement of the right of the press to be as libellous and seditious as it pleases.' In December 1914, the *Times of Nigeria* published an anti-colonialist litany aimed at Lugard: 'From a prancing pro-consul who must have his own way and does not care one iota for the safety of the innocent people under his charge ... From negrophobism, colour prejudice, oppression and deceit, Good Lord deliver us.' It says something for the liberal attitude of British colonial rule that even in time of war press attacks of this sort were tolerated.

At the end of the war, just before Lugard left Nigeria for a busy retirement, he drew up a series of instructions on the duties of political officers. With the people of the south-east in mind, he stated:

> If there is no chief who exercises authority beyond his own village he [the District Officer] will encourage any village chief of influence and character to control a group of villages, with a view to making him chief of a district later if he shows ability.[13]

This attempt to set up a central authority where none had previously existed led to the appointment of Warrant Chiefs who were little more than government agents with no traditional prestige or influence. Here again it was the imposition of direct taxation that finally showed up the weak links in the chain of authority. It was rumoured that women were to be taxed as well as men, and in the dry season of 1929/30, the mysteriously well-organized and militant Ibo women turned out in their thousands to wreck the court houses and beat the government-appointed chiefs. The women thought that the soldiers, sent to quell the riots, would not fire on them, but they were mistaken.

These tragic events were the result of assuming that administrative methods that worked reasonably well in a Muslim autocracy could be applied in very different and little-understood circumstances elsewhere. Serious anthropological study of traditional institutions was at last undertaken. Particular attention was concentrated in certain problem areas such as south-east Nigeria, the Tiv of the Benue and the Ashanti of the Gold Coast. This led to the establishment of elected councils as the unit of local government among the Ibo and Ibibio. When I was travelling through this area in the first year of Nigerian independence, cheery notices were displayed at the roadside: 'Hello, hello, hello. Welcome to Ndor Ebon County Council Area.' And a little further on: 'Ndor Ebon County Council Area – Goodbye.' These cumbersomely styled administrative units had apparently achieved a degree of local patriotism and pride, perhaps more soundly based than the autocracies of the emirates or the Ashanti.

After the First World War, the ex-German possessions in Africa were divided among the victors. The area of Africa under British rule now reached its greatest extent by the addition of Tanganyika in East Africa, and those parts of Cameroon and Togo that were adjacent to Nigeria and the Gold Coast. All were held under mandate from the League of Nations, and once again it was emphasized that this form of trusteeship was a 'sacred trust of civilization' which would continue only until such a time as the territories concerned were able 'to stand on their own feet in the arduous conditions of the modern world'.

In many ways the British West African territories already showed a better chance than most of achieving economic self-sufficiency, although political independence was still some forty years ahead. Revenue derived from customs dues and direct taxation enabled all to pay their way without financial aid from the imperial government. Ownership of land by non-natives was, in general, prohibited, so that primary production of crops for home consumption and export was in the hands of innumerable peasant farmers. Competition such as that provided by Indians and Arabs in East Africa hardly existed in West Africa, leaving much of the internal trade, commerce and salaried employment in African hands, though only the largest of the European exporting firms survived the post-war slump of the late 1920s.

Mining enterprise – iron and diamonds in Sierra Leone, diamonds and bauxite in the Gold Coast and tin and coal in Nigeria – was largely conducted by European companies, as was the export timber trade. The oil wealth of Nigeria was a well-kept secret until Middle East supplies were threatened by the closure of Suez in 1956.

Peasant production had its disadvantages. The traditional West African export crops, palm oil and kernels, were products of palms which grew more or less naturally in the farmlands. Little attempt was made to replace old trees, and today West Africa is importing plantation-grown palm oil from Malaya for local consumption. Cocoa plantations also need more care than most peasant cultivators are prepared to give, and cocoa production is dwindling. But one great advantage which derived from the prohibition of alien land-ownership was that, when the time came, the transition to independence was not complicated by the presence of a European settler population.

THE NEW RECRUIT

Half-way through the sixty years which separated the take-over from the Royal Niger Company and the final granting of independence, the world was in the depths of the Great Depression. Senior Nigerian government officials, on early retirement and retrenchment, were being shipped home by the boatload, but, to everyone's amazement, six newly appointed Forest Officers arrived in Lagos, and I was one of them. A more significant arrival in the same year (1931) was that of the new Governor, Donald Cameron.

The Women's Riots of the previous year had tragically demonstrated the limitations of indirect rule and the difficulty of applying it where local concepts of authority differed widely from European ideas on the subject. Under Cameron, an attempt was made to overcome these difficulties by anthropological investigation and, at the same time, by consulting the growing body of educated African opinion. The idea that government policy should be in any way dependent on African opinion was strongly resented by certain sections of the European community. Cameron was from the West Indies, and it was thought by some that an ethnic explanation must be sought when the British governor of an African colony appeared to favour the aspirations of the indigenous population. As in the days when Roger Casement served in the Oil Rivers Protectorate, it was still thought odd that a colonial official should be 'pro-native' (see plate 69).

In England, by this time, the imperial idea was considered by many to be quite anachronistic, if not definitely deplorable, and I remember trying in vain to think of any of the contemporary literary or political figures whom I admired who would approve of my chosen career.

The romanticized exploits of *Sanders of the River* were currently being celebrated in a lavish film production, but the West End success *White Cargo* had shown the adventurous young Englishman succumbing to the deleterious effects of alcohol and black women, and Noël Coward mocked the 'mad dogs and Englishmen' who went 'out in the mid-day sun'.

But even in this changing climate of opinion, recruitment to the colonial service was no problem. West Africa was still spoken of as the 'white man's grave', but government service offered the then generous starting salary of £450 a year with a week's home leave for every month spent in Africa and a good retirement pension at the age of fifty-five, though statistics used to be quoted demonstrating that the average West African pensioner drew it for only three or four years.

Of course, a system which allowed the employee to spend 25 per cent of such a short working life on leave was most uneconomic, and the normal eighteen-month tour of duty barely gave him time to settle down to the job. But this was the white man's grave.

Africa still offered the prospect of adventure, an outlet for the altruistic missionary spirit and a relatively unexplored field for the inquiring mind. There were still thousands of square miles of hitherto unmapped country to be explored and surveyed; there were unrecorded species of plants, birds and insects to be identified and exotic peoples to be studied.

During the next thirty years, I saw that policy finally implemented which had been stated, in 1865, as 'to encourage in the natives the exercise of those qualities which may render it possible for us more and more to transfer to them the administration of all the governments with a view to our ultimate withdrawal'.[14]

The first thing that struck me on arrival was that, once ashore, there was not a white face to be seen. A fellow recruit and I walked for a mile through the crowded streets of Lagos, from Customs Wharf to Carter Bridge, before we met a white man – a foreman of works supervising bridge repairs – who told us where we could buy a beer. At that time the total African population of Nigeria was probably underestimated at 20,000,000, while white residents numbered some 6,000, more than half of whom lived in Lagos.

I was posted to Onitsha, where I lived in an open-sided, mat-roofed shed with a magnificent view down the mile-wide Niger. At night, the mosquitoes drove me under the net to read Gibbon's *Decline and Fall of the Roman Empire*, which I never finished, or down to the club on my motorbike to drink beer. Coming home, a leopard sometimes leaped across the road in my headlights.

On the roads round Onitsha, droves of well-grown girls were to be seen head-loading yams to market. They wore nothing but strings of waist beads called *jigada* and stacks of brass leg-rings. Sometimes they would be conversing, with no sign of embarrassment, with well-dressed young men wearing shirts and trousers. Girls who attended mission schools wore neat blue uniforms but were stripped naked as soon as they got home, their mothers considering that wearing clothes before marriage led to all sorts of immoral practices. Once independent, most of the Nigerian states passed anti-nudity laws.

The greater part of my first tour was spent at Degema in the Niger Delta. Across the creek at Abonema, small cargo boats used to come alongside, their prows smeared with delta mud and with mangrove branches tangled in the derrick stays, where they had rammed the mud banks negotiating the tortuous bends in the Bileh Creek which led through from the Bonny River. They landed textiles, corrugated roofing sheet, cement, gin and stockfish, and left again with palm oil, kernels and a deck cargo of squared mahogany logs.

The post-war trade boom was over and many of the old trading firms, the Royal Niger Company, MacIver's and Miller Brothers, had been absorbed by the United Africa Company merger in 1929, but the local traders still talked of the lavish entertainment laid on by the wealthy trading chiefs: basins full of 'palm-oil chop', a highly seasoned native dish of chicken stewed in palm oil, and a naked girl standing behind each guest with a bottle of gin.

I arrived in Degema, by steam launch, on Christmas Eve, and celebrations were well under way. On the wide Sombreiro Creek, half a dozen eighty-foot canoes were parading to and fro, propelled by twenty paddlers a side who sent up fountains of spray at each stroke, keeping time with a band of drummers, while the owners of the canoes and their guests could be seen dressed in their best clothes. Cowboy hats, sola topis and toppers bobbed up and down under banners which proclaimed their names: Harry Boy White, Tom West India, Pedro Bob Manuel. Ashore, I was welcomed into a lunchtime gin-drinking session. For the next few days, the sun was veiled in the seasonal harmattan fog and the other senses were dulled by the incessant drumming and the alcoholic haze. 'In Degema,' I was told, 'Christmas lasts from Armistice Day until Easter.'

Across the creek, half sunk in the mangrove mud, lay the remains of the consulate hulk, *The George Shotton*, which had served as administrative headquarters during the last days of the Niger Coast Protectorate at the turn of the century. The figurehead of this old East

Indiaman still stood behind the District Officer's chair, and part of the consulate armament, a three-barrelled Nordenfeldt gun, covered the approach to the rest house. An echo of the days of the palm-oil ruffians still hung about this remote delta port, and even of an earlier period when the creeks had been named Escravos, Forcados and Sombreiro by the Portuguese.

My job was to locate areas of forest suitable for reservation and to check up on European timber exporters and African pit-sawyers and canoe-makers who were required to pay a licence fee on the trees they felled. This fee was supposed to cover the cost of replacing the felled trees, but the department was by no means a net revenue earner. I toured this roadless country by canoe or sometimes with the District Officer in his launch. It was only a year since the Women's Riots, and the Government was attempting to establish local councils that had some sort of traditional basis. I occasionally sat in on meetings at which the District Officer patiently searched for such roots of authority. The village elders with whom he discussed these matters remembered the days of house rule and one or two of them were said to have eaten the Royal Niger Company Kroo boys captured at the Akassa raid less than forty years previously.

When some case of theft, assault or adultery came up, the District Officer would ask the assembled chiefs: 'What would have been the penalty for such an offence before the days of British rule?' He would be told: 'A fine of ten cases of gin or a puncheon of palm oil' or, in extreme cases, 'to be sold to the Aro slave dealers'.

A form of slave trading still persisted in the area. The relative prosperity founded on the delta palm-oil trade was reflected in the high bride-price demanded locally and it was possible to import marriageable girls from impoverished areas up-river at a cheaper rate than that of the local bride-price. Whether a normal marriage was being arranged or whether the girls were actually being bought and sold was not always easy for the District Officer to decide.

A newcomer was inevitably impressed by such sensational relics of a not-so-distant past – nakedness, slave dealing and cannibalism – but it is perhaps unfair to dig them up again fifty years later.

Both government officers and trading agents toured the area to check up on African subordinates at out-stations. At the end of each month they were all back in the station to exchange news of their various activities at the club or office, rather like the managers responsible for different aspects of the running of a large estate.

Europeans filled virtually all the senior appointments in both government and commercial organizations, but, as plans for independence developed, Nigerians were cautiously promoted to posts formerly held by Europeans. Such African holders of senior office were known (in Yoruba) as *oyinbo dudu*, 'black white-man', the term 'white-man' being used as a designation of rank rather than race.

A small squad of African police was attached to the District Officer and a European police officer occasionally visited Degema from Port Harcourt, four or five hours distant by launch. The police were equipped with rifles but did not normally carry them, and the nearest troops were 150 miles away at Enugu. The country was administered peacefully with remarkably little exercise of force, largely owing to the fact that traditional local controls were able to operate within a framework of British administration which was generally felt to be just and reasonable. What could happen when local opinion considered that justice had not been done was demonstrated by the Women's Riots of 1929/30 and the Ochokorocho Massacre of 1946, when an unpopular court decision with regard to fishing rights over a creek near Degema resulted in the slaughter of over a hundred members of the winning side by 'persons unknown'.

European contacts with Africans were mainly of an official nature, although the relationship of master and servant could sometimes be of a rather startling intimacy. An absent-minded and constipated friend of mine, who habitually used the royal 'we' in conversation with his servants, was heard calling to his steward, 'Ojo, have we been to the latrine today?'

Many Europeans enjoyed a happy relationship with a black mistress. If this was not an association of true equals neither was the traditional African marriage, though in both cases the woman could often exert considerable influence on her man.

A probably apocryphal story used to be told of a certain 'secret Circular A', which was issued to all serving government officers, announcing that severe disciplinary action would be taken against officers found to be 'maintaining native women in a state of concubinage'. This resulted in such a serious outbreak of blackmail and anonymous accusations, affecting the whole of government service from top to bottom, that 'Secret Circular B' swiftly followed, stating that, on further deliberation, His Excellency considered that disciplinary action in such cases would be inappropriate.

Many Europeans who have lived in Africa would probably wish to support Richard Lander's tribute when he wrote: 'I take this opportunity of expressing my high admiration of the amiable conduct of the African females towards me; in sickness and in health; in prosperity and adversity – their kindness and affection were ever the same.'[15]

European nursing sisters were recruited but were only posted to headquarters stations. Government officers were not encouraged to bring out their wives. The *Nigeria Handbook* issued to me on appointment stated:

> Every officer is entitled to free furnished quarters ... [but] there is difficulty in providing for all officers quarters which would be suitable for ladies, and the Government accordingly does not permit officers to bring their wives to Nigeria without special permission.

Even if permission were granted, only half the wife's passage was paid. Only missionaries ever brought children out to West Africa, so that any sort of normal family life was unknown until the 1940s, when conditions of service and local amenities improved.

Quinine and other prophylactics dealt fairly efficiently with malaria, but the horror with which the tropical sun was still regarded had been expressed by Kipling many years before:

> 'Who lays on the sword?'
> 'I' said the Sun.
> 'Before he has done,
> I'll lay on the sword.'[16]

But during my time in West Africa, we lost our fear of the sword of the sun.

On my first trip out, I leant over the side of the mail-boat off Freetown to watch the antics of the diving boys, exposing my head to direct sunlight for a moment. An old missionary lady tapped me on the shoulder and warned: 'You're in the tropics now, young man. You must show more respect for the sun.' At mid-day gatherings at weekends, when large quantities of beer passed through the company, in consideration of the limited facilities indoors, it was normal for the male guests to relieve themselves in the garden. But whether it was safe to do so without putting a hat on was a matter of strongly divided opinion. The controversy was finally resolved by the British troops during the war; when out of uniform they discarded their headgear with impunity.

Another health myth that was exploded at this time was that one became 'seasoned' by many years' residence in Africa. A team of Army doctors established that any seasoning process occurred during the first weeks after arrival and depended on the adequate functioning of the sweat glands. This point has already been made in an old song we used to sing about a man dying of blackwater fever that ended:

> And we'll write home and tell his wife
> He could not sweat to save his life.

It was surprising how many kinds of tropical parasites a reasonably fit man could carry round with him without feeling much the worse for it. When I finally left Nigeria, although I felt perfectly well, I went for a general check-up to the Hospital for Tropical Diseases, where they found that I was acting as host to no less than four different kinds of parasite: filaria, hook worm, strongyloides and bilharzia. It was the bilharzia cure that really knocked me out.

To those of us who spent most of our lives in camp or touring from one bush rest house to another, the amenities of piped water, flush latrines and electric light came, at last, with advancing seniority and promotion to office jobs in headquarters stations. But the innovations which affected us all most profoundly were radio communication and air travel. When instantaneous news from Europe and a few hours in a plane replaced the bundle of month-old letters and newspapers and the strange two-week limbo of the mail-boat, the remoteness of Africa was finally abolished.

These developments took place during the war years, when Nigerian troops fought with distinction in the highlands of Ethiopia and the jungles of Burma. Hitler's racist reputation and that of his imitators in Vichy-controlled West Africa encouraged genuine local enthusiasm for this remote European conflict. Led by the black governor of Chad, the French central African territories declared for de Gaulle.

Government officers in Nigeria were all under orders and few saw active military service. I was engaged in promoting the production of wild rubber in an inadequate attempt to make good the loss of supplies from plantations seized by the Japanese. The United Nations charter declared, in cautious terms, an intention 'to promote the progressive development towards self-government or independence as may be appropriate' in the case of the trust territories. Although the Free French Commissioner for the Colonies maintained that 'in the great Colonial France there are neither peoples to liberate nor racial discrimination to abolish'.[17]

But de Gaulle's Franco-African community did not long survive the example of independence achieved by the British West African states, led by the Gold Coast in 1957. Nigeria's size and the mutual suspicions of its ethnically diverse component people delayed the final declaration of independence under a federal constitution until 1960. In the following year Sierra Leone, and in 1965 Gambia, followed suit.

END OF EMPIRE

By the time that Nigeria had actually achieved independence, I had retired from government service, spent six weeks in England where I failed to find work that suited me, and returned to collect traditional art for Nigeria's national museums. Nigeria's political future was uncertain, but her artistic past was of unique distinction in Africa. In consequence, and in spite of legal restrictions, valuable items were vanishing from Nigerian shrines to reappear in the sale rooms of Europe and America, and the Nigerian Government was now making rather belated efforts to divert this flow of antiquities into its own museums.

I had been collecting for about six months when, a week before Independence Day, I returned to the Museum with a vanload of wood carvings, brass castings, pottery and cloth. In Lagos, skyscraper office blocks seemed to have shot up overnight. The lagoon-sided marina had been cleaned up and lined with decorated lamp standards so that it looked like Bournemouth promenade preparing for the season. Across the lagoon, on what had been sandy scrubland and mangrove swamp, rose the concrete bulk of the Federal Palace Hotel and the flimsy structure of the Independence Exhibition. A wide dual carriageway now led out over Five Cowrie Creek to the Federal Palace and on to Bar Beach, where Jolly Boy Bar and the shacks of the small-time prostitutes among the coconut palms had been demolished to make way for a sea-side car park.

Independence had come without a struggle and on the eve of its achievement everyone seemed to be taking it rather quietly. The Southerners in general showed little enthusiasm for the Northern Prime Minister, and only the Ibos were pleased with the appointment of Dr Nnamdi Azikiwe as Governor-General. The Yorubas, awarded no high office, felt themselves slighted. The large population of Ibos who lived and worked outside Ibo-land were definitely apprehensive for their future in an independent Nigeria, and the Tiv of the middle belt were in open rebellion. In the Congo, the crisis over the secession of Katanga was coming to a head, though we were all assuring each other: 'It can't happen here.'

A few hours before the Union Jack finally came down on the Lagos race course, I was sitting alone on the veranda of the Abeokuta rest house, drinking a bottle of beer. The sound of drumming echoed up from the town, there were occasional minor explosions from fireworks or dane-guns and a confusion of sounds from radio loudspeakers playing an often repeated and undistinguished refrain that I finally recognized as the new national anthem: 'Nigeria, we hail thee/Our own dear native land.' 'The end of an era,' I thought, as I opened another bottle of beer. But such a brief episode could hardly be called an era; it was only sixty years since the British Government had taken over from the Royal Niger Company. Yet even sixty years ago it had already announced a policy of 'ultimate withdrawal', so, perhaps, short as it had been, the episode had been unduly prolonged. The bold British businessmen had forced the hand of government, which had been stimulated by colonial rivalry, but the colonial age was already passing. On the eve of independence there were many thousands of Nigerians who had lived to see the British come and go, and I myself had served through half the colonial period.

'You must have seen a lot of changes in your time, Mr Allison.' I suppose I must have done, but it is difficult to judge now what was significant: bare breasts and feet now clothed with Manchester cottons and Bata shoes; corrugated iron instead of thatched roofs; tower blocks and traffic jams; breweries and universities; ten hours in a VC–10 instead of two weeks in an Elder's mail-boat.

I remember the delta creeks; the kernel-strewn trading beaches; the smell of mangrove woodsmoke; the blue-black, crab-infested mud at low tide and the cheerful ribald cries of the grey parrots flying home to roost in the cotton trees along the Sombreiro River. The bat-haunted consulate at Bonny, the rusty ribs of the old hulks along the mangrove-fringed shores of the Brass Sea, where the canoe-perched Bonga fishermen cast their conical nets and the pied kingfishers hover and plunge and the white surf beats on the bar. I remember Christmas at Degema, with the old war-canoes parading up and down the river and the drumming and the harmattan haze and too much gin at mid-day.

I remember camps beside a rock-strewn torrent in the green gloom of the Ondo bush, lying awake beside my girl, Mary, after the first tornado, with the old rotten trees that had been hanging on through the dry season crashing down all around. Head-loading the camp on for a few miles every other week, following up the survey gang until the rains got too heavy and the rivers rose, and coming out to some European company and a pan roof overhead, leaving behind the cleared camp sites with a great wide stick-bed in each, soon to rot away.

In those days, in remote bush villages I used to ask, 'Has a white man been here before?', but now it would be: 'Will a white man ever come here again?' They kept on coming, of course, the post-colonial do-gooders and carpet-baggers ('we're not out here to get our knees brown, you know'), a second scramble for Africa, with everyone joining in this time: Americans, Scandinavians, Israelis, the lot. But most of them would never get further into the bush than the rough on the Lagos golf course.

I remember Sapoba, in the black bush of Benin, looking down into the fathoms-deep, gin-clear water of the Jamieson River with a raft of Obeche logs snaking round Pajeka Island, or curtains of rain sweeping across the wall of the forest beyond. The hand-haulers singing and dancing the logs over the oil-smeared rollers and the axe-men up on a fifteen-foot rickety stick platform, listening for the last fibres to crack, watching for the steeple-high crown to sway and totter, to sweep to the ground, to bounce once and then lie still, while the snowfall of leaves settles and everyone whoops and catcalls: 'One more down and nobody copped it this time.'

I remember Lokoja, the busy river port at the Niger–Benue confluence, the stern-wheelers loading and discharging along the water-front and the empty middle-Niger savannahs behind; the monkeys scampering across the golf course on quiet Sunday mornings and the hyenas grunt-whining round the back of the compounds on chill, dry-season nights, as we sat in unaccustomed sweaters, having one more for the road, outside the European Club under the African stars. Up on the flat, ironstone tableland of Patti, at High Niger, looking down on a line of stern-wheelers bucking the current up the brief Benue flood to Numan, Yola and Garoua. Here, only a hundred years before, sat Consul Baikie, translating the Bible into Hausa and raising a half-caste family, waiting for the boat to take him home to Orkney. When it finally came, he did not want to leave. I did not want to leave either, but nobody had asked me to stay.

Nobody indeed was actually asking us to go. Next morning the Lagos papers announced that all top posts in the Western Region Government still held by expatriates would be taken over by Nigerians, although 'the expatriates would be offered retention on a supernumerary basis'.

The Nigerian press were unanimously friendly and generous. It recalled that, although Dr Azikiwe had once theatened that 'the tree of liberty shall be watered by the blood of tyrants', he had recently conceded that independence had been handed to Nigeria 'on a platter of gold'. One editorial admitted, rather plaintively, that 'after nearly a century of British rule we haven't many scars to show. None of the leaders of the major political parties have been in prison.'

Under these circumstances, a congratulatory message from the Algerian government in exile had a slightly ironic ring: 'The Algerian people, who have been fighting for freedom for the last six years, send warmest greetings to the brother people of independent Nigeria.'

Nikita Khrushchev had written: 'The achievement of independence by your country is yet another indication of the inevitability of the complete collapse of the disgraceful system of colonialism.' But an editorial in the *West African Pilot*, which had always been in the forefront of the journalistic struggle for independence, read:

We are indeed grateful to Britain for leading us thus far and, as she lays her burden and responsibilities down at midnight tonight, we assure the Mother Country that, with the fine training she has given us, we shall do our utmost not to prove a disappointing child.

It was reported that at the official opening of his new palace on Independence Day, the Oba of Lagos announced:

Lagos, apart from being the capital city of the Federation, has some peculiarities of its own. A sceptred isle, like a precious stone set in a silver sea, it has been, since the reign of Oba Ado, the royal throne of obas ... Like a fortress built by nature herself against infection and the hand of war.

The Oba continued in the same style, skilfully adapting Shakespeare's lines to his own purpose and paying unacknowledged tribute to Nigeria's debt to British culture.

It is good to remember these expressions of regret and gratitude with which the press and people of Nigeria saluted the departing British in 1960. Some of the illustrations in this book refer to violent and deplorable events; but on the morning of Nigeria's independence, the colonial wars, the looting of Benin and Kumasi and the enormities of the slave trade seemed to have been forgotten. Perhaps, after a further lapse of time, the depictions of such events can be seen as worth preserving for the sake of the historical record.

II

THE PICTURES

1

═══ THE PIONEERS ═══

The first British adventurers down the Guinea coast, as recorded by their contemporary, the writer Richard Hakluyt, were in search of one thing: profitable trade. In 1553, Thomas Wyndham was buying gold at Elmina on the Gold Coast and then, ignoring the advice of his Portuguese pilot, pushed on down the coast to Benin to load black peppers. Hakluyt reported that as Wyndham waited in the Benin River for the merchandise to be brought down to him, his men,

partly having no rule of themselves, but eating without measure of the fruits of the country, and drinking of the wine of the Palme trees that droppeth in the night from the cut of the branches of the same, and in such extreme heate running continually into the water, not used before to such sudden and vehement alterations (than the which nothing is more dangerous) were thereby brought into swellings and agues: insomuch that the later time of the yeere coming on, caused them to die sometimes three & sometimes 4 or 5 in a day.[1]

Wyndham himself died and his Portuguese pilot was forced by the terrified survivors to put to sea, abandoning the merchants, who were still buying peppers at Benin; 'And of seven score men came home to Plimmouth scarcely forty and of them many died.'

When such stories were told round the dockside pubs of Plymouth and Deptford, the potential profits of such a venture must have been enormous to induce a crew to sign on for another voyage to the Guinea coast.

Ten years after Wyndham's disastrous voyage, Hakluyt recorded that Sir John Hawkins, 'sometimes treasurer of Her Majesties navie Roial',[2] made three trips to Guinea, where 'partly by the sworde and partly by other meanes ... going every day on shore to take the Inhabitants, with burning and spoiling their townes', he collected several cargoes of Negroes. He disposed of them profitably in the West Indies, where, by this time, the Spaniards had been importing slaves for fifty years. The

Spanish Bishop of Hispaniola, Bartolomeo de Las Casas, had urged that the sufferings of the enslaved native Indians should be alleviated by the importation of Africans.

Better-regulated methods, which were accepted as a normal branch of commerce, replaced the kidnapping expeditions of the early slavers. Those who were engaged in the trade were not all sadistic monsters. Nicolas Owen, a small-time exporter of dye wood and slaves from Sierra Leone in the mid eighteenth century, whiled away his time, when trade was slack, with pen-and-ink sketching and shell-work which he learnt from a fellow slaver. 'I have been on board of Captain Engledo today,' he wrote in his diary, 'where I found him making a curious piece of shellwork.'[3] The next day Owen proudly reported on his own efforts: 'I have just finished my shell-work and I think its just shutable [sic] to my dwelling. Its of round form with a looking glass in the middle ... with various kinds of shell and moss taken from the bark of old trees.'

John Newton who, from 1750 to 1754, served as a successful slaver captain, finally retired and took holy orders. He wrote a number of hymns (including 'How Sweet the Name of Jesus Sounds in a Believer's Ear') and was an inspiration to the abolitionist William Wilberforce.

William Bosman, Governor of the old Portuguese fort at Elmina, now in Dutch hands, published (in 1705) a lively account of trading life in West Africa. He suggested that the nearby English fort of Cabo Cors (Cape Coast) was mainly garrisoned by throw-outs from Elmina: 'chiefly sottish wretches, yet they are very welcome to them: the English never being better pleased than when the soldier spends his money on drink ... its incredible how many are consumed by this damnable Liquor (pardon the expression)'.[4] He later admitted excessive drinking was 'too much in vogue' among all Europeans and 'to make quicker work, they are as zealous votaries to Venus as to Bacchus, and so waste the small portion of strength left them from tippling ... and then adieu to Health and soon after Life itself'. He cheered himself up, however, with the thought that 'If men lived here as long as in Europe, 'twould be less worth while to come Hither, and a man would be obliged to wait too long before he got a good post.' Bosman himself had survived fourteen years on the Guinea coast when he wrote his description of Guinea.

The export of slaves – by sea to the Americas and across the desert to North Africa and Egypt – was still at its height at the end of the eighteenth century, when scientific curiosity first prompted exploration of the interior of Africa. The Niger River itself was one of Africa's major mysteries, and when it was discovered that Niger's outlet to the Atlantic was through a maze of delta creeks which had been long known as a source of palm oil, hopes were roused for expansion of a profitable trade up this great inland waterway. But the frightening loss of life on the first trading ventures delayed commercial exploitation of the river until the discovery of quinine as a prophylactic against malaria.

1. Sir Thomas Wyndham, the first recorded Englishman to undertake a voyage down the West African Coast, was painted in 1550 by the Dutch artist Hans Eworth. Three years later Wyndham sailed on his disastrous trading venture to Benin, in the course of which he and nearly three-quarters of his crew died.

△3. Cape Coast Castle (1938). In the late fifteenth century the
Portuguese opened up a profitable trade in gold with the Gold Coast
(now Ghana) that made it worth building substantial stone castles,
many of which are still standing. William Bosman, the Dutch governor
of the fort at nearby Elmina, illustrated some of these in his book, but
complained rather peevishly: 'Death, which spares no man, visited my
draughtsman before he could complete the illustrations.' By Bosman's
time, the main trade was in slaves, and the castles had to accommodate
the human cargoes awaiting shipment.

◁2. This figure of a European musketeer, cast in bronze, was found in
the palace of the Oba of Benin by the Punitive Expedition of 1897,
together with hundreds of brass castings and carvings in wood and
ivory, some of which depicted bearded and armed Europeans similarly
dressed. The musketeer's chain-mail shirt and peaked morion helmet
show obvious similarities to Wyndham's equipment, which help to
date these remarkable brass castings to the sixteenth century.

4. This illustration from Archibald Dalzel's *History of Dahomey* (published 1793) shows a party of British naval officers attending a review of the wives and troops of the King of Dahomey, who is seen seated in the tent. The demands of the transatlantic slave trade stimulated the build-up of powerful slave-raiding armies by the rulers of Ashanti, Dahomey and elsewhere. The King's wives appear to be wearing a rather *décolleté* version of contemporary fashionable European dress, and one of them seems to be repelling the advances made by an officer. The troops in the background are probably some of the much feared women warriors of Dahomey. They were also classified as wives of the King. Since independence, Dahomey has been confusingly renamed Benin.

5. After slave trading was declared illegal for British subjects in 1807, the British Navy patrolled the West African Coast in an attempt to put a stop to the trade entirely. The *Illustrated London News* of 4 April 1849 reported 'a most successful attempt just made by our gallant countrymen towards extirpation of the Slave Traffic, in that infamous hornets' nest of slave dealers, the Gallinas'. The raid was carried out by a flotilla of some twenty ships' boats against a slave shipper's shore establishment on the coast of Sierra Leone.

△6. As late as 28 April 1860 the *Illustrated London News* published this picture showing the capture of a large slaver, off the mouth of the Congo River, by HMS *Pluto*. From the 1840s onwards the ships of the Royal Navy's Anti-Slavery Squadron were increasingly being equipped with steam as well as sail, which gave them considerable advantage in the creeks and coastal waters.

◁7. The early-nineteenth-century explorers were inspired by the pursuit of pure knowledge as well as by the spirit of adventure which has stimulated explorers down the ages. Mungo Park (1771–1806), the tough young Scots doctor, described himself as having 'a general passion for travelling'. He first saw the Niger in 1795 and, ten years later, returned to die in the river before he could trace it to the sea. None of Park's forty European companions survived him, and his son also died in the attempt to complete the work started by his father.

▷8. Richard Lander wore Muslim dress, entertained his companions with tunes on his bugle-horn and flirted with the girls. At his second attempt he reached the Niger mouth in November 1830, a captive in the hands of an Ijaw chief. Two years later, on a trading expeditions in the Niger Delta, he died of gunshot wounds. This portrait is from Lander's *Captain Clapperton's Last Expedition to Africa.*

◁9. Unlike Lander, Mary Kingsley (1862–1900) made no sartorial concessions to the tropics. An explorer and naturalist, she strode through the forests of the Cross River and the Gabon, wearing flannel petticoats and carrying an umbrella. She also died in Africa, nursing Boer prisoners at Simonstown during the South African War.

△10. This illustration from Macgregor Laird's *Narrative of an Expedition into the Interior of Africa* shows one of his side-paddle steamers aground below the Niger–Benue confluence. More serious than such navigational hazards was the appalling death rate among the European personnel, which included that happy traveller Richard Lander.

11. The successful commercial exploitation of the Niger River had to await the discovery of quinine as a malarial prophylactic. This daguerreotype of Dr Willim Baikie, a young Orcadian naval surgeon, was taken in 1854 just before his departure in command of the 'iron screw schooner' *Pleiad*, which was to spend four months in the river without loss of life.

2

——— The Missionaries ———

The missionary enthusiasm which was undoubtedly one of the driving forces behind the early Portuguese voyagers had long been exhausted by the time the eighteenth-century explorers were beginning to extend the knowledge of Africa into an interior which the Portuguese never knew.

Christian priests were attached to some of the larger trading posts and garrisons on the coast to minister to the European personnel, and for many years at the end of the eighteenth century the chaplaincy to the English establishment at Cape Coast Castle was held by an African who had been educated in England.

The humanitarian enthusiasm which had achieved the abolition of the slave trade also gave rise to the evangelical movement in the Protestant churches and stimulated the renewal of missionary activity. In the year before the British abolition of the slave trade, the Anglican Church founded its first West African mission in Freetown, Sierra Leone, to be followed a few years later by the Methodists.

It was necessary that their converts should at least be able to read the Bible. Elementary schools were started and, as early as 1827, the Anglicans opened Fourah Bay College for the training of African clergy. For more than a century of British rule in West Africa, education remained almost entirely in the hands of the Christian missions. In Sierra Leone, the influence of the missions and the education they provided was largely concentrated on the early settlers and the freed slaves, of many different tribal origins, who made up the population of Freetown. Many of these were eager to return to their countries of origin, where their education fitted them for employment as interpreters and clerks. The mission influence spread with them, down the coast to the Gold Coast, Lagos and Abeokuta, where they were known as 'Saros' – a contraction of Sierra Leone.

One of the most remarkable of these Saros was Samuel Ajai Crowther. He was a Yoruba by birth who had been enslaved as a boy and was landed at Freetown from a captured slave ship. He was adopted by a missionary couple and sent to school in England. On his return, he accompanied the early Niger expeditions as an interpreter; later, after ordination, he established a number of mission stations in the delta and up the Niger. He eventually became the first Anglican bishop on the Niger.

A number of the early missionaries were Germans and the Swiss Basel mission was the first to open up on the Gold Coast. The Wesleyans, Anglicans and Presbyterians leap-frogged over each other down the coast to Badagri, Lagos and Calabar. The renewal of Catholic mission activity came later with the awakening of French interest in West Africa.

That interdenominational rivalry was never the fierce issue that it became elsewhere in Africa was probably due as much to the natural tolerance of their congregations as to the Christian forbearance of the pastors. Certainly some of the early Protestant mission publications expressed most unchristian sentiments towards the Jesuits.

The early missionaries were dedicated and courageous people who were prepared to settle in a country still ravaged by slave-catching wars, and were always ready to use their influence to arrange negotiations between the combatants. Not unnaturally, they tended to side with their converts and Thomas Bowen, an American Baptist who had once served as a Texas Ranger, took an active part in the defence of Abeokuta against the Dahomey attack in 1851.

The remarkable Scottish missionary, Mary Slessor (1849–1915), who worked for some forty years in the Calabar area, was appointed a Vice-Consul of the Niger Coast Protectorate on account of her knowledge of, and influence with, the Cross River people.

12. Missionaries accompanied the earliest Portuguese explorers and, 400 years later, the first Niger expeditions. Among these was Samuel Crowther, the freed slave, who established schools and mission stations in the river and its delta. He is seen here rather overtopped by a collection of religious carvings which were surrendered to him by Chief Ockiya of Brass, after the Chief had been converted to Christianity. These particular carvings appear to have been shipped back to mission headquarters in London. But many similar ones were destroyed by fanatical converts, both Christian and Muslim. Today, many Christian churches in West Africa are adorned by sculptors working in the traditional manner.

13. A group of missionaries in the more salubrious climate of the Yoruba country, at Abeokuta (about 1870). The Reverend Townsend (seated at centre) first visited Abeokuta in 1842 at the invitation of a group of freed slaves who had made their way back from Freetown. The early missionaries, including Wood and Mann (standing second and third from the right) successfully gained the confidence of the local people and were instrumental in negotiating a cease-fire in the Yoruba wars, which were supplying the cargoes for the last years of the slave trade.

14. This photograph of Mary Slessor (1849–1915) seems to have been taken when she was on leave in Scotland, probably in the 1890s, and shows her with Janie, Mary, Alice and Maggie, some of the children she adopted to save them from death. In the Cross River area, twins were traditionally regarded as an abomination who should not be allowed to live. Mary Slessor is best remembered for her fight against this inhuman practice.

15. In the early days, the Protestant mission was one of the few places where one might catch a glimpse of a young white woman. Captain Bower, the first Resident Ibadan – with a fellow officer – are calling on the mission ladies, perhaps with a view to inspecting the attractive new recruit (on the right) before the climate gets at her.

16. Mission school children and their teachers at Charlotte School, Freetown (1880s). Christian missions were often established in advance of the colonial administration and provided the beginnings, not only of education, but also of medical services.

3

═══════════ TRADE ═══════════

During the early part of the nineteenth century palm oil was increasingly becoming a necessity; it oiled the wheels of industry and, in the form of soap, washed away its grime. 'The famous yellow soap of Old England' the Victorian traveller and journalist Winwood Reade called it, and, thinking of the mortality among West Coast traders, he added dramatically, 'every bar contains a drop of English blood'.[5]

The creeks of the Niger Delta had been known as the Oil Rivers before their connection with the great river was suspected. Originally the trade had been carried on much as in Wyndham's day: the ship would anchor in one of the estuaries – Calabar, Bonny or the Nun – and wait until local traders brought down sufficient cargo by canoe. Later, buying agents were established on the hulks of the old ships anchored in the creeks which, until conditions improved, were considered safer and more healthy than living ashore.

When navigation of the Niger by wood-burning steamers became possible, there were hopes of a great increase in trade, but to begin with the results were disappointing. Already groundnuts were being exported from French Senegal and the Gambia, and eventually, when transport facilities by river, rail and road improved, the cultivation of groundnuts spread throughout the dry zone of West Africa and the tonnage exported outstripped that of palm oil and kernels. The most valuable crop from the high rainfall areas was cocoa, and by the 1920s the world demand for this product was largely being supplied from West Africa.

In the days before the African producers of palm oil had been fully absorbed into the cash economy, the old traders used to say, 'the higher the price the lower the heave', meaning that the demand for cash and imported goods was so limited that it could be satisfied by bringing a lower tonnage for sale when the price was high. But luxury imports were soon seen as necessities and the imposition of direct taxation eventually created an annual demand for cash.

The peculiar trade tokens of an earlier age – brass rods, cowries and manillas – lingered on in small-scale market trade. Manillas (see plate 25) were finally bought in by the Nigerian government as late as 1948. But from the beginning of the colonial period, the trader paid out cash for palm produce and expected to get a fairly high proportion of it back in payment for the imported goods he offered for sale to the producer. Indeed, at many small stations the buying and selling points were under the same roof and there would be no competition.

A variety of European manufactures eventually found a ready sale in Africa, but by far the most important of these, by value, was cotton cloth. Hand-weaving of cotton cloth was a well-developed home industry throughout much of West Africa, but it was a laborious process and the bright colours, light texture and cheapness of the machine-woven cloth ensured its popularity. For certain purposes, however, the products of the hand-loom continued to be in demand.

The early palm-oil trade was founded on the European demand for soap, lubricants and butter substitutes, but the expansion of that trade was stimulated by the need of British industrialists to sell their cotton goods. The seventies and eighties of the last century was a period of economic slump, with the cotton trade in particular suffering from overproduction. Manufacturing interests repeatedly urged government to open up new markets in Asia and Africa, and in 1884, on the eve of the Berlin Conference, the *Journal of the London Chamber of Commerce* called upon commercial interests 'to prepare public opinion and the government of the country for a new colonial movement from which alone a revival of trade can be expected'.[6] In British West Africa, commerce did not wait on government action: the new colonial movement was inaugurated by George Goldie and his Royal Niger Company.

By 1929 the trade was dominated by Lever Bros., the soap manufacturers, who had bought out the Niger Company and a number of other competitors to form the United Africa Company. As well as taking care of the buying of the natural crop, Lever Bros. had looked ahead to ensure future supplies and proposed to establish oil-palm plantations. The Nigerian Government refused to allow them to acquire land for this purpose, and the plantation scheme was transferred to the Belgian Congo.

Government had opposed the alienation of land for plantations on the grounds that it would be in the best interests of the country that production should be left in the hands of the peasant farmers, and that they should not be transformed into plantation labourers. However, no steps were taken to regenerate the semi-natural palm groves which were the source of the oil. Production dwindled and today palm oil, even for home consumption, must be imported from plantation-grown palms in Malaya.

17. Buying palm oil by the calabash in the Niger Delta (about 1895). The annual export of palm oil and kernels from Nigeria alone amounted to some 400,000 tons at the end of the Second World War. This tonnage was still almost entirely collected from palms growing naturally in the farms and was bought in the exiguous quantities seen here.

18. The men who bought the palm oil (about 1895). Trading and shipping agents at Bakana, a port in the eastern Niger Delta, later to be superseded by Port Harcourt. This was a fairly large European community, but much of the buying was done at one-man stations further up the creeks, where the only relaxation would be with a local girl and the gin bottle. The beautiful and mysterious lady in the spotted veil was probably the agent's wife. She looks, understandably, as if she wishes she was elsewhere. The stairs in the background lead up to the 'top', as living quarters over the office and store were called.

19. 'Chop ready' on the 'top' of the Elder Dempster shipping agent at Bakana. The large tureen on the table probably contains palm-oil chop – a popular, highly seasoned country dish of chicken stewed in palm oil. In those days the provision of five 'boys' to wait on half a dozen 'masters' would not have been considered excessive. A hand-operated punkah hangs from the ceiling to keep the diners cool. Beer would be drunk with the meal, and wine glasses were probably intended for gin, which was considered necessary to 'settle' a plate of palm oil.

▷20. John Holt's trading factory at Bansara, on a tributary of the Cross River. The agent lived in his 'top' over the store; behind are the kitchen and 'boy's' quarters; in front are the puncheons of oil ready to be shipped down to the port of Calabar, some 160 miles distant. Water transport was essential to allow the cheap movement of this bulky product to the port of shipment.

▽21. Chief Abbeys of Bonny entertains his business associates (1905). Social relations between European traders and the African middlemen with whom they did business were normally very relaxed and cordial. In compliment to their host, the Europeans have replaced their trousers with native dress, referred to as 'lapper' or 'arse cloth'. Much of the produce shipped came through big African traders such as Chief Abbeys, who had ramifying contacts up-country who ultimately bought from the producer. Such trade networks centred on the old slave ports of Bonny and Calabar had been in operation for generations.

▷22. A Lagos trading store in the 1930s. Here the money paid out to the producer found its way back to the buyer. In the 1950s more than a third of the total value of imports into West Africa was accounted for by cloth, mainly cotton goods; a long way behind came motor vehicles and bicycles.

23. The groundnut pyramids of Northern Nigeria: bagged groundnuts await transport
to the coast by rail (late 1940s). As soon as road and rail transport developed,
groundnuts became the main export from the low-rainfall areas of West Africa. A
tonnage equal to that of palm-oil and kernels put together was produced on
innumerable small family farms of a few acres each. At this time part of the crop
was brought to the railhead by the camel-load.

▽24. Attempts at large-scale mechanized production of groundnuts in the late 1940s were a failure in both East and West Africa. Steam-traction engines, used in a groundnut scheme at Minna (Nigeria), were abandoned in the bush.

▷25. In pre-colonial times, a variety of local currencies were in use: brass rods, cowries and these metal hoops, known as manillas. Manillas were in use from the late fifteenth century onwards and were being manufactured in Birmingham up to the end of the nineteenth century. In Southern Nigerian villages they were still accepted in the 1940s. They were eventually bought in by the Government in 1948/49, at £1.00 for eighty.

26. A raft of squared mahogany logs in the Siluko River, Nigeria (about 1910). When the raft was made up, the African raftsmen kept the logs moving, by tide and current, to the ports of Lagos and Sapele for export to Europe. In the days before mechanization, the logs were hand-hauled over rollers to the nearest floatable water. Four miles was generally considered to be the maximum economic hand-hauling distance. As the economy developed, timber was increasingly converted in sawmills and plywood factories in Nigeria and Ghana for local use.

4

═══ WARS ═══
AND EXPEDITIONS

The European merchants on the coast wanted only to be left in peace to carry on their profitable trade in slaves, gold, ivory, palm oil or whatever product was in demand at the time. Successful trade was largely dependent on establishing mutually satisfactory arrangements with African trading agents on the coast, and on the Gold Coast friendly trading communities had grown up under the protection of the European forts.

Towards the end of the eighteenth century, however, the powerful Ashanti Federation began to dominate the surrounding tribes from its capital of Kumasi in the high forest more than a hundred miles inland. The Ashanti had long been primary producers of gold and slaves, and now, in an attempt to benefit more directly from the profits of the coastal trade, their well-organized armies began raiding down to the area protected by the forts. Here they came into collision with forces led by Europeans who were attempting to defend their trading partners. The Ashantis frequently came off best in these engagements and, in 1824, defeated a force led by Sir Charles M'Carthy, the Governor of the British West African possessions, whose head was carried back to Kumasi to adorn an Ashanti war drum.

Repeated raids of this sort resulted in an official British proposal to abandon all her West African possessions, except Sierra Leone. In the event, however, it was the Dutch and the Danes who withdrew, and the British were left in command of all the forts. Once again the Ashanti army crossed the Pra River, which was the recognized boundary of their territory, and the British Government was at last spurred to decisive action.

Previous British forces had consisted of a small body of trained garrison troops, supported by large numbers of unreliable local irregulars. For the Ashanti War of 1874, some 2,500 British troops were assembled, supported by a detachment of the West India Regiment, local constabulary and the usual native auxiliaries, all under the command of Sir Garnet Wolseley, the military man of the moment. This heterogeneous force entered Kumasi after some hard fighting, but the difficulty of head-loading up supplies over some 120 miles of bush paths necessitated an almost immediate return to the coast.

Before final annexation as a crown colony in 1900, two further military operations were mounted against the Ashanti. Such persistent and effective opposition to British advance was encountered nowhere else in West Africa, though before the end of the century two tough but brief actions were fought in what is now Nigeria.

The punitive expedition against Benin could hardly have been avoided. J.R. Phillips, the acting Consul-General of the Niger Coast Protectorate, proposed a friendly visit to the Oba of Benin. The Oba asked him to postpone the visit, but Phillips set out with his unarmed party and was attacked on the road. He and six of his European companions were killed, along with many of the African carriers accompanying them.

Retaliation came with remarkable speed little more than a month later: a force of seven hundred blue-jackets and marines and four companies of Protectorate troops were assembled and a week later entered Benin. Here indeed the evidence seemed to justify the overthrow of the old régime: the town reeked of the wholesale human sacrifice which had been performed in an attempt to enlist superhuman intervention against the British advance.

As the naval force fought its way through the forests of Benin, the first assault on the Fulani emirates was being mounted by the Royal Niger Company Constabulary, some two hundred miles to the north. The Company had found that trade through its river ports was being disrupted by periodic slave raids by the emirs of Bida and Ilorin, and, in a campaign which lasted little more than a fortnight, a small force of the Company's Constabulary, under British officers, achieved results which the British press compared with Clive's victory at Plassey.

27. The Ashanti War of 1874 was one of the few incidents in West African history that captured the attention of the British public and even inspired a piece of popular music, the Ashanti March, and a *Punch* cartoon. Concanen's cover to the Ashanti March shows British and West Indian troops landing at Cape Coast in preparation for Sir Garnet Wolseley's rather less than glorious march to Kumasi.

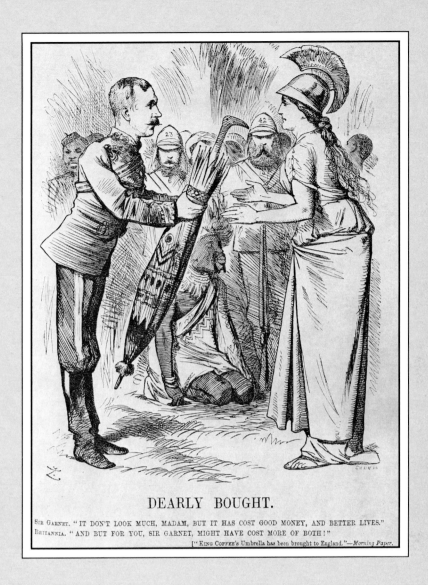

DEARLY BOUGHT.

SIR GARNET. "IT DON'T LOOK MUCH, MADAM, BUT IT HAS COST GOOD MONEY, AND BETTER LIVES."
BRITANNIA. "AND BUT FOR YOU, SIR GARNET, MIGHT HAVE COST MORE OF BOTH!"

["KING COFFEE's Umbrella has been brought to England."—*Morning Paper.*]

◁28. Melton Prior, special artist for the *Illustrated London News*, accompanied the campaign. He was known as 'the screeching billiard ball' on account of his high-pitched voice and bald head. The road to Kumasi was stoutly and efficiently defended. A quick-action sketch by Prior shows British troops and African stretcher bearers under fire from an Ashanti ambush. As Sir Garnet marched into Kumasi, the inhabitants and defenders fled into the bush and he found himself master of a deserted town, which he vacated again after only thirty-six hours. It was impossible to keep his troops supplied at such a distance from the coast.

◁29. Two hundred and fifty blue-jackets of the Naval Brigade accompanied the expedition. In this picture from the *Illustrated London News* they are seen making themselves comfortable in an Ashanti courtyard.

△30. The *Punch* cartoon suggests that the Ashantehene's umbrella – presented to the Queen – was the only form of indemnity collected. In fact, considerable quantities of gold-work were looted from the palace and the Ashantehene's envoys chased the retreating Sir Garnet with a propitiatory gift of 1,000 ounces of gold. The British public found it quite hilarious that an African potentate should be called King Coffee (more correctly, 'Kofi'). He is fancifully depicted in the background, along with figures representing the Black Watch (42nd), the Welsh Fusiliers (23rd) and the Gold Coast Hausas. The expression 'all Sir Garnet', meaning 'all in order', seems to have originated from this campaign, but Sir Garnet himself referred to it as 'the most horrible war I ever took part in'.

31. This picture of the Bantama, the mausoleum of the Ashantehenes, was probably taken during a friendly visit to Kumasi in the 1880s. Many of the West African kingdoms practised human sacrifice, and scenes such as this convinced the British that the overthrow of such régimes was a moral obligation.

32. By 1895, the British were more actively concerned with staking out claims in a West African hinterland now threatened by French and German colonial expansion. An offer to the Ashantis of protection by Her Majesty the Queen was politely declined, and once more British troops landed through the surf at Cape Coast, where they were photographed by Major Robert Baden-Powell (later hero of Mafeking and founder of the Boy Scouts). Beards and puggarees were no longer the fashion, but Sir Garnet was still remembered by the 'Wolseley pattern' sun helmet which was to be standard issue for another forty years.

◁33. This time the only deaths on the road were from disease and heat-stroke and the troops entered Kumasi unopposed, to the strains of 'Home Sweet Home', played by the Hausa buglers. But the Ashantehene (Prempeh), together with members of his family, was abducted and exiled to the Seychelles, where he remained for thirty years before returning to Kumasi.

◁34. One of the major problems of the Ashanti campaigns was that of keeping the troops supplied with thousands of cases of bully-beef and other foodstuffs over 120 miles of bush-path through dense tropical forest. The carriers and their loads are assembled at Cape Coast Castle, ready to accompany the Expedition of 1900, which relieved the Governor of the Gold Coast, who was besieged in his own fort at Kumasi.

The Ashanti presented the toughest and most persistent opposition to British advance into the interior, though armed operations aimed at keeping trade routes open, and later to forestall colonial rivals, occurred sporadically throughout the area. Powerful chiefs had become accustomed to manipulating the flow of trade to the coast for their own profit, and naturally resented any infringement of their monopoly. In Sierra Leone, one such clash of trading interests resulted in the Bandajuma Expedition of 1889. A series of photographs survive which record the progress of this typical 'little war'.

△35. A detachment of Sierra Leone police and their white officers parade at Jehomah, ready to march on the village of slave-raiding chief Makaia of Lago.

△36. The assembled 'war boys' (as warriors were termed in Coast pidgin) of two chiefs (Gbanah Gumbo and Momoh Jah) who were prepared to support the British force, for reasons of their own. Four days later, Makaia had fled and his village was burnt. It is recorded that large numbers of women and children who had been enslaved by him were freed and sent home.

▷37. An immediate response to the Benin Massacre in 1897 was obviously essential. A bare six weeks after the event, in fact, blue-jackets and marines of the Cape Squadron were in action against Benin outposts: a remarkable achievement since the ships had to be summoned from stations in the Atlantic as far apart as Simonstown and Gambia. A week later, Benin had fallen and this unsuspected wealth of brass castings and carvings in ivory and wood were found in the Oba's palace. This was claimed as a form of indemnity and was subsequently sold off by auction in London. The value of such a collection in the sale-rooms today would be enormous. The line of demijohns probably contained palm wine, no doubt emptied on the spot by the thirsty troops.

38. The *Daily Graphic* of 9 April 1897 illustrated the attack on the Royal Niger Company square outside Ilorin, from a sketch done on the spot. Lieutenant Burdon, who was present, commented: 'This is a very fair picture of the charge except that the cavalry did not come on in such a dense mass ... and the horses are too big.'

39. Machine-gun drill: Northern Nigeria (about 1900). As Hilaire Belloc commented at the time:

> Whatever happens we have got
> The Maxim gun and they have not.

The square was formed by the riflemen standing at arm's length from each other, with a machine-gun mounted at each corner. These were the tactics that defeated the courageous horsemen of the Sudan at Bida, Ilorin, Sokoto and Omdurman.

5

GAMBIA:
THE RIVER BANK COLONY

B ritain's earliest, and topographically oddest, West African possession consisted of a strip of land averaging about ten miles
deep on either bank of the Gambia River. The early European
adventurers had hoped to intercept the trans-Sahara gold trade from the
upper reaches of the river, and the early-seventeenth-century English
trader, Richard Jobson, brought back curious tales of the 'silent trade'.
The Moors of Barbary dealt with mysterious gold producers who were
so shy that they refused to meet strangers face to face but were much
in need of the salt that the strangers could supply. On the banks of a
certain river, the Moorish traders left piles of salt and then retired out
of sight. When they returned, they found that a pile of gold-dust had
been left in place of the salt, or if the salt had not been removed the
trader knew that he must add more, if he wished to do business.

Jobson returned with many strange tales but very little gold. When
Mungo Park set off on his Niger quest from a trading post on the
Gambia, salt was still in demand and small quantities of gold were still
available, but the main export was now slaves.

By the mid nineteenth century, when Richard Burton and Winwood
Reade visited the river, the trade had settled down to the export of
groundnuts, which continues to be Gambia's main hard currency earner.
According to Reade, British administration of the territory was based
mainly on an annual trip up the river by a boatload of officials from
the capital, Bathurst: 'Every year the Governor or his deputy ascends
the river, encourages the kings and chieftains with words and presents
to protect the traders and attempts to settle any disputes.'[7] Along with
some officers of the West Indian regiment, a Wesleyan missionary and
the Chief Justice, Reade joined this annual expedition to MacCarthy
Island, of which Burton had caustically remarked: 'this butt-end of the
habitable world ... derives its name from Sir Charles M'Carthy,
whilom Governor of Sierra Leone, who in 1824, by the mistake of
his ordnance-keeper in bringing up biscuits and macaroni instead of
ammunition, was beheaded by the Ashantis'.[8]

This narrow corridor of territory maintained an equally narrow economic equilibrium by reason of its navigable river, which attracted the trade in groundnuts from an area far beyond its political boundaries. Even after the end of colonial rule, Gambia retained its independence for nearly twenty years before forming a union with the (ex-French) Republic of Senegal which surrounds it. This is one of the few instances of the old colonial boundaries being revised since independence in West Africa.

Gambia has one of the nearest stretches of tropical sea-coast to Western Europe, and tourists can now enjoy a trip up the Gambia in the wake of Richard Jobson under pleasanter conditions than were suggested by Richard Burton.

40. The original caption reads: 'Palaver opposite
MacCarthy Island, 1891'. This was probably taken on
the occasion of the annual tour of his charge made by the
Governor of Gambia, as described by Winwood Reade:
'The picture suggests colonial administration in a
pleasantly relaxed atmosphere; the Governor arrives in
his comfortable yacht and settles palavers under a shady
tree; unfortunately, according to Burton, MacCarthy
Island was "a hot-bed of disease".'

41. G.T. (later Sir Gilbert) Carter with his wife and
daughter (about 1885), when he was Post Master and
Administrator of Gambia. Family life of this sort was
rarely enjoyed by Europeans in West Africa at this time,
and may have contributed to Sir Gilbert's longevity. He
lived to draw his pension until the age of seventy-nine.
When Governor of Lagos (1891–7), he extended British
rule into the Yoruba country with remarkably little use
of force.

6

═══════ SIERRA LEONE: ═══════ COLONY AND PROTECTORATE

Some twenty years after Gambia had been taken from the French as spoils of war, twenty square miles of Sierra Leone were bought from a local chief. Here the original 'black paupers', freed by the Mansfield judgment, were landed. A few years later they were joined by a boatload of American Negroes who had sided with the British in the War of Independence and had then been unhappily settled in the harsh climate of Nova Scotia. The Maroons, a community of escaped slaves who were deported from Jamaica, also ended up in Sierra Leone.

These early settlers were soon vastly outnumbered by the human cargoes landed from the captured slave ships arrested by the Royal Navy's Anti-Slavery Squadron which for some sixty years was based at Sierra Leone. At most the Squadron consisted of twenty ships and 1,000 men: all too small a force to patrol the thousand-odd miles from the Senegal to the Congo, from which slaves were still being shipped. The 'recaptives', as they were called, came from an even wider area, and the Reverend Koelle, an early missionary, reckoned that 150 distinct African languages were spoken in Freetown. Many of the early settlers had no previous contact with Africa and evolved their own form of English, known as Krio, which became the spoken language of the Colony and – in the form of pidgin English – the lingua franca of much of the coast, including the German Cameroons where the Catholic missions published a *Pidgin English Child's Bible History*.

The area around Freetown, which was declared a crown colony in 1808, was governed under a constitution similar to that granted to other crown colonies, such as Canada. Freetown, where nearly half of the senior government posts were at first filled by Africans, had a mayor and alderman, and civil cases were tried by jury. This application of British standards of justice to an African colony scandalized such Victorian travellers as the negrophobic Richard Burton, who was briefly British Consul at Fernando Po in the early 1860s. He commented: 'The British Constitution determines that a man must be tried by his peers', and then briefly and disparagingly listed the sort of 'peers' he might have been tried by in Sierra Leone.[9]

Freetown was, for many visitors, their first sight of Africa and some, like Burton, did not approve of what they saw. Scenically, the Freetown peninsula is certainly the most attractive stretch of the coast: steep, forest-clad mountains sweep down to sandy coves and lagoons; villages of clapboard and whitewashed mud, with names like Waterloo, Leicester and Regent, emerge from groves of banana, mango and breadfruit, the whole scene and its inhabitants more reminiscent of the West Indies than of Africa.*

Until the 1870s the Governor of Sierra Leone was responsible for the administration of all the British West African territories, but until the end of the century little attempt was made to extend his authority northwards. When Travelling Commissioners were appointed to make treaties with the chiefs of the Protectorate, it was realized that the French advance from Senegal was seriously limiting such expansion. Perhaps Sierra Leone would have done better, territorially, under an energetic commercial enterprise such as the Royal Niger Company.

To the north the French had come into collision with the Mandingo warlord Samory, who had been in the habit of importing his armaments through Freetown. When hard pressed by the French, Samory offered his allegiance to the British, but, under Colonial Office instructions, Governor Hay turned the offer down and helped the French to drive Samory westwards to the north of the Gold Coast, where he was captured and deported.

An injudiciously early attempt in 1898 to collect Hut Tax in the Protectorate resulted in serious armed resistance, which appears to have led to a reluctance on the part of the administration to interfere with traditional institutions of any kind, and domestic slavery was not legally abolished in the Protectorate until 1928. It is indeed ironical that, in a British colony which was founded as a home for freed slaves, any form of slavery could have been tolerated for so long. The majority opinion among the Colony population was opposed to abolition, as they feared that it would result in an influx of freed slaves into Freetown. In fact, the Commissioner of the Central Province reported: 'The abolition of the legal status of slavery came into force on the first of the year [1928] and was received with calm bordering on indifference.'[10]

Much of the internal trade, which in the Gold Coast and Nigeria was in African hands, was taken over in Sierra Leone by Syrians and

---

* My memories of Freetown are forty years out of date.

Lebanese. This lack of local enterprise may well have been due to the apathy induced by the conditions of slavery.

The oil palm grows naturally throughout the country, due to the generally high rainfall, and the development of an export trade in palm products was encouraged by the early construction of a railway into the Protectorate, initially as far as the town of Bo. According to a local song, 'The train for Bo 'e no fit go'; technical hitches may, at first, have been frequent.

During the 1930s the discovery of iron and diamond deposits considerably increased the value of exports, though a diamond industry in the hands of a monopoly has inevitably encouraged a disruptive smuggling industry.

For more than 150 years the citizens of the Colony had been encouraged to regard themselves as an élite community, and the prospect of being transformed into an unpopular minority, after freedom from colonial rule, was understandably disturbing. The final pre-independence general elections inevitably resulted in victory for the Protectorate Party, which wisely formed a United Popular Front to lead the country into independence in 1961.

△42. A Mende village in Sierra Leone (about 1880). The stockade would be protection against the slave-raiding 'war boys' of Makaia (see p. 74). The British brought stability to this country, though sometimes by violent means. The men in uniform are members of the Sierra Leone Frontier Police.

◁43. T.L. Aldridge was one of the first Travelling Commissioners who toured the country north of the colony, and concluded treaties which led to the declaration of a protectorate. He appears here, ready for anything, with armed escort, a hammock and a canoe-puller. The early administrators were normally recruited from members of the armed services, but Aldridge had come out to Sierra Leone as a trader. He collected ethnographic information and material, including a number of remarkable stone carvings, known as *nomoli*, now in the Museum of Mankind.

44. (overleaf) Here is Aldridge again, riding in his hammock, though rather an austere, two-manpower model. The picture gives a good idea of a bush-path through high forest, emerging into a village clearing with banana trees.

45. Kissi Street, Freetown (about 1905). The *pax Britannica* had been established for a hundred years: a policeman walks his beat, the street has a London lamp-post and even an ice-cream cart.

46. The Freetown Hill Station was a sort of suburban Simla where, after 1900, on the recommendation of Sir Ronald Ross, the authority on malaria, European quarters were built in a healthier climate a few hundred feet above the town. The lamp-post and the station architecture must have reminded the English exiles of home. The rather dejected-looking figures are probably Europeans' cooks, waiting for the train to take them down to Freetown market. When motor transport became available, about 1912, the Hill Station railway was dismantled.

△47. The citizens of Freetown assemble to bid 'Farewell to Our Highly Esteemed Governor, Sir Leslie Probyn' (about 1904). They were loyal British citizens and, in common with their white fellow citizens of the day, thought themselves rather better than the next man. The mail-boat to take the Governor back to England lies out in the bay

▷48. By 1910 Freetown had qualified for a royal visit. To avoid unnecessary exertion and exposure to the climate, the Duke and Duchess of Connaught were met at the quayside by twin hammocks with canopies, from which they inspected a guard of honour mounted by the 2nd Battn. of the West India Regiment, not yet replaced by West African troops.

▷49. In the grounds of Government House, the wives of prominent citizens are presented to Her Royal Highness in 1910.

7

========= GOLD COAST =========
TO GHANA

The Gold Coast was the first West African state to achieve freedom from colonial rule and at independence assumed the name of the ancient Sudanese empire of Ghana, which had flourished, around the sixth century, almost a thousand miles away to the north-west.

Ghana assumed an illustrious name with little historical justification, but its actual history has differed significantly in several respects from that of other West African territories. The climate of the Gold Coast was relatively salubrious, the trade in gold was regular and valuable, and the anchorages were so unprotected that, from the fifteenth century onwards, the traders found it preferable to establish permanent shore stations. These stone-built castles housed a regular garrison and trading staff who lived in close contact with the local African communities.

The forts changed hands – the Portuguese were replaced by the Dutch, the English and the Danes – but along this stretch of coast permanently staffed trading posts proliferated at a time when, elsewhere, trade was being hurriedly conducted from ships briefly anchored in pestilential creeks and estuaries.

By the time that Government took over the British forts, no satisfactory alternative had been found to replace the now illegal trade in slaves, such as was provided by palm oil in the Niger delta. The slaves had been brought down the coast on their own feet but, although gold was sufficiently valuable to stand the high cost of head-loading, the Gold Coast rivers were generally unsuitable for transporting the bulky, low-value palm products. Cask roads were constructed along which palm produce was expensively rolled in barrels, but difficulties of trade and transport and the disturbance caused by Ashanti raids finally led to the withdrawal of the Dutch and the Danes, and the British found themselves in possession of all the Gold Coast forts.

Long association with them had introduced the Fante, of the western coast, to many European ideas and institutions, and when it appeared that the British would leave, along with the Dutch and the Danes, the Fante chiefs proposed to form a self-governing federation, with an elected president, to regulate their own affairs and organize defence against the Ashanti. When these proposals were referred to the British Governor, he considered them to be seditious and arrested the delegates, though they were subsequently released. Three years later, after the Ashanti War of 1874, the British declared the southern Gold Coast to be a British colony. Ashanti and the northern territories remained nominally independent until 1901.

Five years after the Gold Coast became a British colony, a plantation labourer, Tetteh Quarshi, returned from the Spanish island of Fernando Po with a handful of cocoa beans, and the country's economic future was transformed. By 1911 the value of cocoa exported had surpassed that of gold, and ten years later the Gold Coast was supplying half the world's cocoa consumption. Large areas of unfarmed land suitable for cocoa were available, and the world price of cocoa continued to rise. Railways and motor-roads replaced the old cask roads, and a deep-water port was opened at Takoradi. By the early years of this century, this was by far the wealthiest of the West African territories per head of its relatively small population.

Culturally the population was remarkably homogeneous, compared with Nigeria, and a well-educated and politically conscious élite formed an influential element in the coastal towns. These factors, combined with the prosperity founded on gold and cocoa, made the Gold Coast an obvious candidate for early independence, which was achieved in 1957.

The cautious colonial government had amassed considerable financial reserves, and the cocoa price continued to rise. The optimistic new government of Ghana inaugurated costly schemes of industrial development based on a hydro-electric scheme on the Volta River, the exploitation of bauxite deposits and a second deep-water port. The world cocoa price continued to rise during the year after independence, but over the next three years it sank to half its 1959 level. The results for the first independent West African government were catastrophic, and President Nkrumah blamed a neo-colonialist conspiracy for this financial disaster which struck so relentlessly at the newly independent Ghana.

Colonial governments have been criticized for encouraging export crops at the expense of food production. In general, British West African governments appeared to follow an agricultural policy of *laissez-faire* and the introduction of the cocoa crop in particular was entirely due to African enterprise.

◁50. A British envoy at the court of the Ashantehene Kwaku Dua, who reigned briefly during the period of weakened central authority which followed the war of 1874. In 1885, when this picture was taken, the Governor of the Gold Coast colony was attempting to renew peaceful contacts with the Ashanti to counteract French and German influence from the west and east. The British attempt to offer 'protection' from these threats led to further hostilities in 1895. The Golden Stool, symbol of Ashanti unity, is mounted on its own chair to the Ashantehene's right.

◁51. A bivouac on the road to Kumasi. Perhaps the same envoy as in the previous plate rests beside the bush-path, with his armed escort and bugler. Kumasi was surrounded on all sides by dense high forest. It was on this forest soil that the cocoa crop flourished which was to become the wealth of Ghana.

△52. Celebrations at Cape Coast for the coronation of Edward VII, 1902. One more military expedition against the Ashanti had been required to relieve the Governor of the Gold Coast, who was being held prisoner in his own fort at Kumasi. But by Coronation Day, Ashanti had been annexed outright and all was well-ordered jubilation, at any rate in the streets of Cape Coast, with parades of schoolchildren and friendly societies. As in London of the period, the straw boater was in fashion.

53. Mr Edwin Powis and his wife, prospecting for gold along the Ancobra River (1910). In the following year, the value of cocoa exported exceeded that of gold for the first time, although gold exports continued to increase.

54. The Legislative Council of the Gold Coast (1919). At a very early stage, the West African territories were provided with legislative councils which consisted of the Governor (Sir Gordon Guggisberg, in this case), certain officials (here, wearing uniform) and a number of nominated unofficial members who represented commercial and local interests (wearing suits and native dress). The official membership remained in the majority until after the Second World War, and even then the unofficial members were predominantly nominated by the Governor. It was intended that the legislative councils would eventually evolve into an elected parliament.

55. The Prince of Wales visited West Africa in 1925. Compared with the Connaughts'
visit to Sierra Leone in 1910 (see plate 48), it seems to have been a remarkably
informal occasion. The Prince manages to produce a slightly nervous grin when
confronted by a masquerader in the course of a 'walk-about', probably in Accra.

56. Ghana's wealth: harvesting and extracting the beans from the cocoa pod. In the
early days, cocoa was produced on innumerable small family farms alongside the
food crops, but, as the industry prospered, farms tended to increase in size and paid
labour was employed. Major buyers of the crop in Ghana and Nigeria were the well-
known confectioners Rowntree, Fry and Cadbury.

8

NIGERIA: THE FIRST FIFTY YEARS

It was a raid on a slave port in 1851 which led to the founding of the Colony of Lagos, which, during the century that followed, expanded and ramified to become the oil-rich giant of West Africa.

In the course of the wars which accompanied the break-up of the Oyo empire, large numbers of Yoruba slaves were taken who were shipped out through Lagos during the dying years of the now illegal trade, mainly bound for Brazil. During December 1851, a British naval action resulted in the replacement of the slave-dealing chief Kosoko by his rival Akitoye, who was prepared to support the British in their attempts to abolish the trade. Ten years later, with the reluctant agreement of Akitoye's successor, Lagos was annexed as a British colony.

The new colony was at first administered as a dependency of Sierra Leone and then of the Gold Coast, but the Colonial Office was firmly opposed to any further expansion. Governor Glover was reprimanded for having annexed some villages to the west of Lagos, but pointed out to the Secretary of State that no very definite direction on the subject had ever been given to him: 'The only instruction I remember to have received from Your Grace was "we have got war, obtain for us peace".'[11]

Glover is usually credited with raising the locally recruited Lagos Constabulary, though it was one of his predecessors who recommended the replacement of the West Indian garrison by local troops on the grounds that 'they require no commissariat, little or no transport, and nourish themselves on the products of the country... Wearing no shoes they do not get footsore on long marches.'[12]

Glover and his Lagos Constabulary played a decisive and dramatic role in the Ashanti War of 1874, but he was shortly afterwards posted as Governor of Newfoundland: perhaps with the aim of cooling his sometimes inconvenient ardour.

An independent Governor of Lagos was appointed after the Berlin Conference of 1885 had stimulated the staking out of colonial claims. When the French occupied Dahomey, it was thought expedient to revive some of Glover's neglected annexations to the west of Lagos and to extend protection over the major Yoruba states of Abeokuta and Oyo to the north. This was achieved with remarkably little opposition from the war-weary Yorubas. Only the Ijebus resisted the interference with their control over the main up-country trade route.

To the east, beyond the Niger Delta, the Germans were beginning to exert pressure from Cameroon. British consuls, appointed by the Foreign Office, had been posted to the Spanish island of Fernando Po to look after the interests of the palm-oil traders in the Oil Rivers. The traders themselves had made some attempt at commercial control through locally constituted Courts of Equity, whose members consisted of the most important traders, both black and white, in each area.

The Consul now moved his headquarters to Calabar, on the mainland, and the area was proclaimed as the Oil Rivers Protectorate. An armed constabulary was recruited, and vice-consuls were posted to the various rivers which formed the only lines of communication in the territory. Here, according to the local fashion, they were accommodated on hulks moored in the waterways.

The major extension of its authority carried out by the Niger Coast Protectorate (as it came to be called in 1893) was the occupation of the Benin country which followed the punitive expedition.

At the end of the century, Nigeria was composed of a peculiar jig-saw of authorities: the Colony of Lagos, under the Colonial Office, which exercised an ill-defined protectorate over the Yoruba country; the Niger Coast Protectorate, under the Foreign Office; and the whole of the vast interior was nominally administered by George Goldie's Royal Niger Company.

◁57. Croquet at Government House, Lagos. The top-hatted figure on the extreme right is probably Sir Alfred Moloney, the first independent Governor of Lagos. Such parties consisted of a thorough mixture of guests, of all colours and occupations, with enough missionaries to act as interpreters between those who had no common language.

◁58. A ramshackle guard house (known as British Agege) on the creeks to the west of Lagos, delimited the extent of the British authority in the direction of French-occupied Porto Novo. The jaunty figure on the left is probably Governor Moloney again: still in top hat and morning dress, though touring to the limit of his charge. To the right is Fred Evans, his Colonial Secretary. Samuel Johnson, the Yoruba historian who knew him, said that Moloney seldom travelled far from Government House and was 'too fond of writing letters to, and drafting treaties for, men who hardly appreciated the one or comprehended the other' (*History of the Yorubas*, Lagos, 1937, p. 613).

△59. Lagos Marina, from the tower of Christ Church. The Governor's yacht, *Gertrude*, is moored at Government House jetty. The Governor could tour his charge on a system of tidal creeks that stretched all the way from French-occupied Porto Novo to the German Cameroons. Until Carter Bridge was built in 1900, Lagos was cut off from the mainland: an island in a land-locked lagoon.

△60. Stimulated by the Berlin Conference, and the French reaction to it, the Colonial office sanctioned a more expansionist policy, and several of Governor Glover's earlier annexations were now ratified. At Igbessa, west of Lagos, the flag is raised over a collection of thatched huts in a banana grove by Acting Governor George Denton (about 1891).

▷61. Acting Governor Denton, in a boater on a treaty-signing visit to Ado in 1891.
The town of Ado had originally appealed for protection against the 'Amazons' of Dahomey; when the French occupation of Dahomey had removed this threat, Lagos felt the French presence to be a more serious menace and concluded treaties with a number of communities along the Dahomey border.

▷62. The Lagos Constabulary parading with their band, artillery and mounted officers – one black, one white. They were generally known as the Lagos Hausas, but, as well as Hausa speakers from the North, Yorubas from the Lagos hinterland were also recruited. This was said to make the most satisfactory combination: the Northerners showed more dash and aggression in combat, while the Yorubas were steadier and more reliable in holding operations and garrison duties.

◁63. Once the road through Ijebu Ode had been forced, penetration of the Yoruba country was remarkably peaceful. In 1897, Governor McCallum took his wife on tour up-country. In the small tent on the right the Governor appears to be working late at the office. A palm-leaf roof has been erected over the tents for added protection from the sun.

◁64. The Consulate Hulk at Sapele in the Benin River. Here, to the east of Lagos, the Niger Coast Protectorate was administered by consuls appointed by the Foreign Office. There was little dry land in the delta, and both traders and government officials occupied 'hulks' moored in the creeks. These consisted of the hulls of old ships, protected from the weather by thatched or corrugated iron roofs. In the foreground is the state canoe of the Jekri chief Dore (more correctly spelt Dogho). He was a trusted agent of Government in the area and was responsible for rescuing survivors from the Benin Massacre which took place in 1897, the year after this photograph was taken.

△65. Even when it was possible to build on dry land, the influence of hulk architecture persisted, as is apparent from the Bonny Consulate decorated for Christmas Day Sports (1900).

△66. Up the Sombreiro River at Abonema, young Captain Bartwell, the Vice-Consul, appears perfectly confident of his ability to deal with the venerable local Kalabari chiefs, who, in their turn, are also no doubt confident of their ability to deal with Captain Bartwell. On Bartwell's right hand sits Chief Young Briggs. The people of the delta had been trading with Europeans for some three hundred years and many of the local names had become anglicized.

▷67. Chief Horsfall's state canoe, off Degema (1904). Such canoes, pulled by some twenty-five men a side, could be used to transport half a dozen puncheons of palm oil or, mounted with cannon, to attack a trade rival. Anyone able to man a canoe of this size was recognized as a chief by both the local community and the British who, until 1914, administered the country through such 'heads of houses'.

▷68. Captain Bartwell's headquarters was the *George Shotton* hulk, moored off Degema. According to Bartwell's assistant, the hulk accommodated quarters for Bartwell, his assistant and a doctor, also a court-room, offices and space for fifty prisoners below decks. Ashore there was a vegetable garden and a tennis-court. The small turret on the roof was known as a 'gin-and-bitter tower'; here the occupants could enjoy the evening breeze while taking their sundowners.

69. An historic group photograph taken at Calabar (probably about 1895). Seated on
the right is Major (later Sir Claude) MacDonald, Consul-General for the Niger
Coast Protectorate (1891–6); between him and his wife sits Mary Kingsley, explorer
and naturalist. On the left of the back row is Ralph Locke, one of the two Europeans
who survived the Benin Massacre two years later. On the right is Roger Casement,
of whom a fellow officer said: 'We call old Roger "the black man's friend" . . . he is
what some people call "pro-native"' ('Nemo', *Niger Memories*, Exeter, 1937).
Casement had a distinguished career in the Foreign Service in South America and
Africa, and was knighted in 1911. During the First World War, however, he considered
that he would be doing his best for Ireland by collaborating with the Germans
against the British Empire and was hanged as a traitor.

9

JUBILEE YEAR

As the century drew to a close, the mounting enthusiasm for the new imperialism culminated in the celebration of Queen Victoria's Diamond Jubilee in 1897. In the previous year, Colonial Office rule had been extended to the interior of Sierra Leone, and once more, British forces had entered Kumasi – this time under attack only from heat-stroke and tropical disease.

Early in the year of Jubilee, the Royal Niger Company Constabulary, accompanied by Sir George Goldie in person, had routed the forces of the slave-raiding emirs of Bida and Ilorin, and a force of blue-jackets had occupied Benin, referred to, with reason, as the 'city of blood'. Kitchener's army (with the assistance of Thomas Cook, the travel agent) was moving up the Nile to the defeat of the Mahdi, which was completed in the following year at Omdurman. It almost looked as if these spectacular actions had been saved up for this auspicious year.

Fifty thousand imperial troops from all parts of the Empire assembled in London for the celebrations. And among those who paraded through the City to attend the thanksgiving service at St Paul's was a contingent of Royal Niger Company Constabulary and their officers, who had actually been in action against the Fulani cavalry a few months before.

Lieutenant Burdon made a scrap-book of that memorable year, which included photographs of the advance from Lokoja, a plan of the battle-field at Bida and invitations and dance programmes from the celebrations in London, which included a special performance at the Lyceum Theatre of Henry Irving in *The Bells*. Lieutenant Festing, who sketched the action at Ilorin, rode through the streets of London on his pony, Rifleman, which had won at the celebratory race meeting held at Bida after the victory.

After a banquet in Manchester, Major Arnold, who had commanded the troops, was reported as saying, 'Every step forwards in that country on the Niger was attended by the reflection that it was another little work done for Manchester ... of infinite importance to the trade and traders of his native city.' If ever it were true that trade follows the flag, the reverse was certainly the truth in West Africa: trade carried the flag up the Niger, and battles were fought, not for Queen and Country, but for the cotton kings and mill-owners of Manchester.

The *Manchester Courier* wrote of the 'immense market the victory will open up for the trade of the country'. Even the *Church Missionary Society Gleaner* commented that 'now the Niger Company have conquered the whole territory there is an opportunity for a new era of prosperity and for mission work'.

Only in the *Liverpool Journal of Commerce* did the Company's competitors ask indignantly: 'How can the position of the Niger Company be justified? Have the Emirs of the Niger ever molested any of its officials?' But this almost solitary note of disapproval was obviously sounded by envious trade rivals.

The French were moving down the Niger and had occupied Bussa (where Mungo Park had met his end), but the imperial trouble-shooter Frederick Lugard was back from a temporary appointment in Bechuanaland and would take care of that threat. Nothing could be allowed to cast a shadow across the Jubilee summer of 1897, though only two years later the Empire was to be plunged into the abysmal gloom of Black Week at the beginning of the Boer War.

70. A group of officers from the various colonial armed forces assemble in London for the Diamond Jubilee celebrations of the summer of 1897. The only West African included is Lieutenant Dan Bornu of the Gold Coast Hausas, and his face is half hidden by the head fourth from right in the row next to the back. Fourth to the left of Dan Bornu, wearing a dark spiked helmet, is Lieutenant Burdon, who fought in the action against Bida and Ilorin; he also made up the scrap-book which illustrates the part he played in this eventful year. The photograph was taken at Chelsea Barracks and includes officers from Australia, Canada, the West Indies, Ceylon and Malaya, as well as West Africa and elsewhere.

◁71. Colonial troops marching past St Mary-le-Strand on their way to the thanksgiving service at St Paul's. At the centre, the double files reading from the rear are composed of: Lagos Hausas; Sierra Leone Frontier Force; Royal Niger Company Hausas; and Gold Coast Hausas (wearing white spats).

△72. Jubilee celebrations at Lagos included joy-rides for local chiefs on the railway that had opened the previous year, and was now advancing towards Ibadan: surely a remarkable gesture of confidence in a little-known and sparsely administered country. In the following years Lagos was lit by electric light, though, to judge by conditions fifty years later, it was probably wise to keep a paraffin lamp handy.

△73. Jubilee medals were presented to co-operative chiefs. The one illustrated belonged to the Amapetu of Mahin, a territory on the coast to the east of Lagos.

74. Towards the end of this year of celebration, at a judicial inquiry held at Benin, the British satisfied themselves that the Oba (Ovonramwen) had not been directly responsible for the massacre of 1897. He was, however, deposed and is seen here, a pathetic and bewildered figure, under guard on board the protectorate yacht *Ivy*, on his way to exile in Calabar.

75. Meanwhile, the settlement of the Yoruba country was proceeding remarkably peacefully. At about this time, Olowe, a master carver of Ise Ekiti, depicted the visit of an early administrative officer to an Ekiti chief.

10

═══════ LUGARD ═══════

At the height of the Jubilee celebrations news came that the French had occupied Bussa and were threatening the Royal Niger Company territories further downstream. Chamberlain, at the Colonial Office, sent for Captain Lugard.

The Royal Niger Company could not be left on its own to deal with another European power. Lugard was promoted to the rank of Brigadier General, and he returned to the Niger, in a hurry, to raise the West African Frontier Force for the defence of this non-existent frontier with the French. A similar confrontation was threatening across the other side of Africa, at Fashoda on the Nile. For a time war seemed inevitable.

It was impossible to complete the raising and equipping of such a force at short notice, but Lugard was on good terms with Goldie and, to begin with, was able to make use of the Company's resources. Recruitment was started through the Company's military establishment at Lokoja, and its flotilla of river steamers was available for the transport of troops and equipment.

Lugard mistrusted Chamberlain's 'chess-board' policy, which involved occupying any villages on the disputed frontier not actually garrisoned by the French; but the matter was eventually settled without military action, although Lugard suspected that a small body of French African troops who had been tricked into handing over a French post to the British were probably shot by their own officers.

Such international complications, an approaching clash with the Muslim emirates and complaints of monopolistic practices by commercial competitors, both black and white, all indicated that Company rule could no longer be tolerated. When confronted by some of these accusations, Goldie had bitterly remarked: 'An Imperial

◁76. On the left, wearing an informal straw boater, is William Wallace, Agent-General of the Royal Niger Company, from whom Lugard (right) took over as High Commissioner for the Protectorate of Northern Nigeria. Wallace continued to serve as Deputy High Commissioner for the next ten years. The type of wooden house on concrete pillars, seen behind, was still known as Lugard House when I lived in one at Lokoja in the 1940s.

Administration may steal a horse while a Chartered Company may not look over the hedge.'[13]

This uneasy period of dual control lasted for a couple of years, and then, on the first day of the new century, at Dr Baikie's old station, Lokoja,

the Company's flag was hauled down: the Union Jack was run up; the guns fired their salute; the African military band played the National Anthem and the black troops gave three hearty cheers for the new and, to them, quite unimaginable sovereign.[14]

Lugard, now High Commissioner of Northern Nigeria, soon found that the authority of the Company did not, in fact, extend much beyond the banks of the Niger and Benu. Almost immediately he had to send all his available troops to the relief of the Governor of the Gold Coast, besieged in his own fort at Kumasi, and could not afford any sort of military action. Chamberlain had indeed warned him: 'We must not have another native war,' but Lugard was another example of the ambitious and energetic man-on-the-spot, prepared to override instructions from a Colonial Secretary who, in this case, perhaps, only half expected to be obeyed.

As soon as the troops returned from Ashanti they were dispatched to deal with some of the lesser Fulani emirs, beginning with that inveterate slave raider the Emir of Kontagora. When it had been suggested to him that he should cease from raiding, he had dramatically responded: 'Can you stop a cat from mousing? When I die I shall be found with a slave in my mouth.'[15]

Peaceful overtures were made to the paramount Muslim ruler, the Sultan of Sokoto, who replied: 'Between us and you there are no dealings except as between Mussulmans and Unbelievers: War, as God Almighty has enjoined on us.'[16] The campaign against the emirates which followed was brief but decisive. The same battle order as at Bida and Ilorin – square formation with Maxims at the corners – was not so effective in the forests of Ashanti and Benin but deadly in the open savannah country.

Meanwhile, fifty miles to the north of Sokoto, an Anglo-French boundary commission was dividing up the spoils of an unfinished conquest. The French, oddly enough, seemed satisfied with a settlement which awarded them a million square miles of desiccated sahel and desert. At the time of the settlement, Lord Salisbury had sarcastically referred to the area as 'What a farmer would call very light land', adding, 'we have given the Gallic cock an enormous amount of sand, let him scratch in it as he pleases'.[17] At that time no one suspected that there might be something worth scratching for under the desert sands.

When Lugard returned in 1912 after five years in Hong Kong, it was as Governor-General designate of a unified Nigeria, but also to conduct a colonial war which had spilled over into Africa from a European conflict.

Colonial rivalry was one of the complicated factors leading up to the First World War, and, a few months after the amalgamation, Nigeria found itself at war with the German territory of Cameroon on its eastern borders. A combined force from the Gold Coast and French Dahomey quickly occupied German Togoland, but the campaign against Cameroon continued for another two years.

Despite the fact that the Sultan of Turkey had sided with the Germans, the leaders of Muslim opinion in West Africa all proclaimed their loyalty to Britain. But much to the surprise and disgust of the British, the people of Cameroon supported the Germans with equal loyalty until their forces retreated into the Spanish territory of Rio Muni.

A Nigerian brigade then served in the East African campaign which, owing to difficulties of communication, continued after hostilities in Europe had ceased. Lugard, with pardonable pride in the regiment he had himself raised, wrote to his wife: 'There is no doubt that the Nigerians won the campaign.'[18]

After his retirement in 1919, Lugard stated his practical and straightforward theory of Europe's dual mandate in Africa: 'to bring the material and moral benefits of European civilization to Africa and at the same time make available to the rest of the world Africa's trade and resources'.

77. The stern-wheeler *Empire*, landing troops and stores at Jebba (1900). First commissioned as a cargo steamer in 1896 by the Royal Niger Company, *Empire* saw service in a variety of roles in the early days in Northern Nigeria. In 1897 she formed part of the armed flotilla which prevented a large Nupe force, caught raiding south of the Niger, from returning to the defence of Bida. She also transported troops and supplies for the newly formed West African Frontier Force (WAFF) during the confrontation with the French, and again in the course of the campaign against the Fulani. In 1902, after their wedding at Madeira, *Empire* carried Lugard and his bride (Flora Shaw, *The Times* colonial correspondent) on their honeymoon up the Niger to Lokoja.

78. The WAFF medical service organized by Lugard was described by him as being 'somewhat large and elaborate'; it included not only two field hospitals and four doctors, but also 'three lady nurses'. Three young white women up the Niger in those days gave rise to some problems, but their presence was obviously appreciated by their patients, and they later all received decorations. The picture is captioned 'Nursing Sisters: Nutt and Powell, Restoring Two Patients to Health. Hospital Jebba, W[est] A[frica], 1898'.

◁79. The official caption to this photograph merely states that it was taken by Captain C.H.F. Abadie in 1903. Captain Abadie was Lugard's Political Officer during the Fulani Campaign of 1903, and the centrally seated figure in a white suit and with a large moustache must be Lugard. But between March and early April 1903, Lugard personally received the submission of Kano, Sokoto and Katsina, completing a journey of nearly 800 miles, on foot and horseback, in thirty-eight days. So it is not easy to pin down the location of this photograph.

◁80. Large numbers of slaves were liberated during the occupation of Northern Nigeria, many of them mere children. They were temporarily lodged in Freed Slaves' Homes, such as this one at Maifoni, Bornu, where (about 1904) they are seen exchanging the rigours of slavery for those of military discipline. The small boy on the right is displaying a fine spirit of rugged individualism.

△81. In 1912, after five years in Hong Kong, Lugard returned to West Africa, where he was to become Governor-General of the combined Protectorates of Northern and Southern Nigeria in 1914. Upon his return, he presented the prizes at Lagos races: a small man with a commanding presence, he is easily picked out as the centre of attention in the crowded stand. A race course was an invariable feature of the British centre of administration. Horse racing was an interest which could be shared by both the governors and the governed, and a winning horse bestowed prestige on black and white alike.

82. A combined French and British force invaded Cameroon in 1914 and, with naval support, the main port, Duala, was taken a few months after the opening of hostilities. Lugard and General Dobell are landing at Duala in November 1914 from the Governor-General's steam yacht, *Ivy*. The guard of honour is composed of African troops: French on the left and British on the right. Hostilities continued up-country for more than a year.

83. Troops of 2nd Battn. Nigeria Regiment in trenches. It seems rather surprising that trench warfare, on the pattern of the Western Front, should have featured in this fluid African campaign.

11

THE VOYAGE OUT

In the old days you were liable to be dumped into a surf-boat at Accra; or into a tender alongside the mail-boat, rolling in the open roadstead outside Lagos bar; or perhaps trans-shipped at Forcados to finish your journey pounding up the Niger in a stern-wheeler. But when I first knew it, the mail-boat berthed in a civilized manner, at any rate at Takoradi, Lagos and Port Harcourt.

For the first few days out of Liverpool, passengers emerged reluctantly from smoking-room and saloon to tramp briefly round the wind-swept, heaving decks. But once clear of the Bay of Biscay, the sun shone, the canvas swimming-tank was rigged on the forward well-deck, and, after the Canaries, flying-fish skittered away over the sea from the ship's prow.

Acquaintances were renewed with people whom one probably met only on the mail-boat, because postings, both government and commercial, tended to be territorial, and one became more or less permanently attached to a single territory or region.

For many, the centre of life on board was the smoking-room. Here, in the early 1930s, the presence of ladies was barely tolerated, and enormous brass spittoons under the tables were mementoes of a less refined age. The bar was opened before breakfast for those who came up in dressing-gowns to start the day with brandy and gingers. From about 11 o'clock the ice-cold Wrexham lager was flowing, and by the time the lunch gong sounded, enormous trays of pink gins were rushed about the decks to keep customers going when the bar closed, and they would eventually be obliged to go down to the saloon for lunch.

It was customary to complain of the mail-boat's cuisine, but, in fact, the food was good and varied, and included such Lancastrian specialities as hot-pot, black puddings and tripe. Apart from eating and drinking, there were rather rudimentary facilities for deck games, and dancing in the evenings, with never enough ladies to go round. In the First Class, dinner jackets were worn, though seldom used during the rest of the tour.

At Madeira or Las Palmas, in the Canaries, you could see the last of Europe – with a Portuguese or Spanish accent. A few days later came the first sight of Africa, usually at Freetown: a jumble of corrugated iron roofs at the foot of steep, forested hills. Here, black boys came out in canoes to dive for pennies, and ashore there were sandy, casuarina-shaded bathing beaches.

At Takoradi the mail-boat docked, but at Accra goods and passengers were spectacularly landed into surf-boats. And then, on to Lagos in its landlocked lagoon; steaming along the green shores of the marina with its whitewashed buildings and coconut palms to the Customs Wharf and Apapa and the worst day of the tour; suddenly stepping off the boat into real life; haggling your way through the customs (perhaps to be introduced to the husband of your shipboard sweetheart); trans-shipping a pile of crates and tin trunks on to the branch-boat to Port Harcourt or up-country by rail or road; to come to rest at last at your station where, with luck, you would be welcomed by the familiar grin of your steward, prepared again (within his limited capacity) to organize your comforts (with the inadequate materials at hand) for the next year or two until, once again, you set out on the long voyage home.

In those days we spent a fairly high proportion of our service on the mail-boats: a strange limbo of shipboard life suspended between Europe and Africa; a time of brief and easy friendships and flirtations; a month of idleness, but absolved from guilt because you were all the time in motion, not actually working, certainly, but travelling to and from work by the only means available.

Then came air transport: dinner over Europe, breakfast over the Sahara and back in your station by teatime. Africa was no longer dark and remote, which must have been a good thing.

◁84. The last sight of England: Liverpool Pier Head and the Liver building (about 1939). Elder Dempster's mail-boats used to sail from Prince's Dock (off left), which is today used only by the Isle of Man ferry. Liverpool docks, like many others, are now mainly of interest as a marine archaeological site.

◁85. A group of officers and saloon passengers on RMS *Axim* outward bound (late 1896). The only member of the group named is Lieutenant Thompson (second from the left). He had been seconded from the regular army for service with the Royal Niger Company Constabulary and was the only European killed in the action against Bida a few weeks later. The presence of the solitary black lady is unexplained, but the saloon passengers on any West African mail-boat usually included some well-to-do Africans.

△86. The first sight of an African for many first-timers: diving boys off Freetown, waiting for passengers to throw down some coins.

△87. At Accra and the other surf ports on the Gold Coast, ships had to lie about a mile or so off the shore, with goods and passengers loaded on to surf-boats. The crew of paddlers took the boat in on a wave, hauled it through the surf and man-handled both cargo and passengers ashore.

▷88. Cargo and passengers were lowered into the boat by the ship's derrick; passengers were accommodated in the 'mammy chair', the inference being that a man would normally go over the side by the rope ladder. This picture was taken in 1908. The flimsy-looking wicker chair was later replaced by a stoutly built wooden box which seated four.

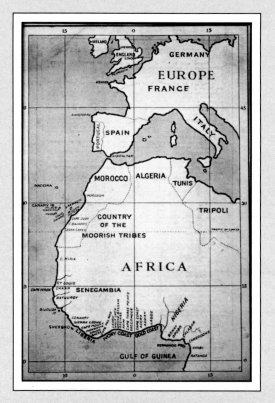

◁89. Passengers in Elder Dempster's boats between the wars will remember this map, which was displayed on the ship's notice board, with flags which were moved to indicate the ship's position at noon. A sweepstake on the day's run provided a little excitement and stimulated bar sales. The romantic suggestion of a wild country inhabited by Moorish tribes was still valid, because although a trans-Saharan bus service was operating by the early 1930s, the pacification of southern Morocco by the French was only completed at about the same date.

◁90. Even a large canvas bag full of sea water, rigged in the forward well-deck, was a welcome amenity when the weather warmed up. When the ship rolled, the water in the tank washed over the side into the sea and could have carried an incautious bather with it. There was not much opportunity for swimming, but it gave the lady passengers a chance to display their bathing costumes.

△91. Many completed the voyage out by rail. Ilorin (1938) is a mainline stop on the way north from Lagos. A large Yoruba town, it was conquered by the Fulani early in the nineteenth century, and was also the scene of the Royal Niger Company action in 1897. The dress and customs of their Muslim overlords were adopted by the Ilorin Yorubas.

△92. The anonymous calm of the departure lounge at Lagos air terminal, twenty years later, seems a world away from the busy African chaos of Ilorin Railway Station.

▷93. 'All visitors ashore please.' After a rapid turn-around, the boat prepares to leave Apapa once more for Liverpool (about 1938). The lucky homeward-bound passengers will shortly be enjoying what used to be known as 'the best view of Lagos' – from the stern of a homeward-bound mail-boat.

▷94. The first air-mail to arrive in Nigeria flew via Khartoum and landed among the camels and Kanuri horsemen on an improvised landing-strip at Maiduguri in 1934. Passenger services were not in regular operation for another ten years. Only those who remember the days before air transport shrank the world have experienced Africa as truly remote.

12

=========== IN THE BUSH ===========

There are degrees and grades of bush. After a couple of months in camp, surveying a remote forest area with only the labour gang and my servants for company, I had to go into a small headquarters station to draw money to pay the labourers and replenish the stores. This involved a two-day trek and a canoe journey of five or six hours. I stayed over the weekend, enjoying some European company, iced beer and cold-store food before returning to bush. On Sunday, a European from Lagos, sixty miles away, brought his new wife out to show her what 'the bush' was like. One man's bush can be another man's high life.

Preparations for going to bush started months before we left Old England's shores. Tropical outfitters were anxious to sell us everything we might need, and a lot of other things as well. Cholera-belts were no longer worn, but I bought a bush-shirt which had buttons down the back for fixing a spine-pad: an extra strip of quilted khaki drill which some thought necessary to protect the spine from the rays of the sun.

Camp-bed, table, chairs and bath were a necessity, as you might be quartered in a bush house consisting of four walls and a roof, or sent off to camp. If you were not allocated a house, you could claim 'bush allowance' but, owing to the financial stringency of the 1930s, bush allowance was stopped just after I arrived in the country.

Junior Foresters and Surveyors normally spent the dry season in bush, living in a tent and trekking with carriers. In the high forest areas, the dry season usually lasted about six months: November to April. It was convenient for the department and personally preferable for Junior Foresters to take leave during the rains, which meant that we usually took home leave every other summer.

There was a certain amount of double-talk about 'going to bush'. No one wanted to admit that he didn't enjoy it. After all, young men came to Africa for a life of adventure, and there was nothing adventurous about living in a house with electric light and running water and sitting in an office all day. The people who really did enjoy it were the amateur anthropologists and naturalists, which included the hunters and the fishermen. As is often the case, those who were most knowledgeable about animals were the ones who enjoyed hunting them.

Presumably owing to the relatively dense human population, wild life in West Africa has never been as plentiful as in East Africa. Indeed, many East African species have never occurred in the West. Even in 1830, when the Lander brothers walked from Badagri, on the coast, to the Niger, they recorded seeing only monkey and hippopotamus, and those on only a few occasions. A hundred years later, a hunter had to walk a long way and work very hard if he wanted to shoot elephant, buffalo and the larger antelope and carnivores. Not a thing I ever wanted to do.

National parks and game reserves were belatedly created by the colonial governments and should ensure the preservation of the surviving indigenous wild life. Conservation, as a tourist attraction and currency earner, is now popular with African governments.

David Livingstone wrote of 'the mere animal pleasure of travelling in wild unexplored country'.[19] A century later there was little of such country left in Africa, but enough to give us a taste of what he meant. We could not hope, like Jobson (up the Gambia in 1623), to see 'one small bird, which for his strangenesse we observe, he hath no legges'.[20] Or 'another strange bird there is which flyeth with four wings'. But there were still strange and unrecorded plant and animal species to be observed, though you had to be something of an expert naturalist to recognize them.

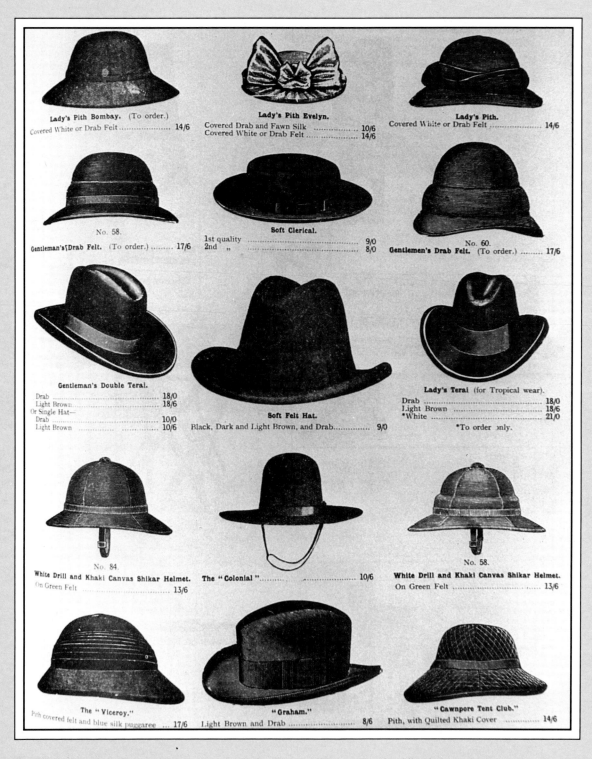

Lady's Pith Bombay. (To order.)
Covered White or Drab Felt 14/6

Lady's Pith Evelyn.
Covered Drab and Fawn Silk 10/6
Covered White or Drab Felt 14/6

Lady's Pith.
Covered White or Drab Felt 14/6

No. 58.
Gentleman's Drab Felt. (To order.) 17/6

Soft Clerical.
1st quality 9/0
2nd „ 8/0

No. 60.
Gentlemen's Drab Felt. (To order.) 17/6

Gentleman's Double Terai.
Drab 18/0
Light Brown 18/6
Or Single Hat—
Drab 10/0
Light Brown 10/6

Soft Felt Hat.
Black, Dark and Light Brown, and Drab.............. 9/0

Lady's Terai (for Tropical wear).
Drab 18/0
Light Brown 18/6
*White 21/0

*To order only.

No. 84.
White Drill and Khaki Canvas Shikar Helmet.
On Green Felt 13/6

The "Colonial" 10/6

No. 58.
White Drill and Khaki Canvas Shikar Helmet.
On Green Felt 13/6

The "Viceroy."
Pith covered felt and blue silk puggaree 17/6

"Graham."
Light Brown and Drab 8/6

"Cawnpore Tent Club."
Pith, with Quilted Khaki Cover 14/6

95. I started off with a Wolseley pattern (rather like that illustrated as the shikar helmet). I graduated to something more dashing like the gentleman's double terai and thence to an ordinary single felt. Eventually, following the example of the off-duty soldiers in the 1940s, I discarded headgear entirely.

SPECIALISTS IN
TROPICAL · CLOTHING

WHITE & KHAKI DRILLS, TUSSORES, ALPACA, PALM BEACH, etc.,

EXTENSIVE RANGE OF STYLES
AND SIZES ALWAYS IN STOCK
READY FOR IMMEDIATE WEAR
OR
MADE TO ORDER.

HELMETS, BUSH SHIRTS, MOSQUITO NETS, UNDERWEAR, CAMP FURNITURE, Etc.

ILLUSTRATED CATALOGUE
FREE ON REQUEST.

Our Tropical Outfitting Department is in the charge of an Expert Staff who have had Practical and Residential Experience in the Tropics.

BENJAMIN
BREWSTER
LIMITED.
53 & 55, BYROM STREET,
LIVERPOOL.

96. I once owned a Palm Beach suit but never managed to look much like this. This picture was an advertisement in the *Nigerian Handbook* (1929).

◁97. Going to bush in comfort. In the early days, elaborate headgear and a long-sleeved jacket, reinforced with a thick spine-pad, were considered necessary for protection against the sun's rays, while a flannel cholera-belt was worn to avoid stomach chills. Wrapped up in this way in the hot wet climate of West Africa, physical exercise was most unpleasant and might have caused heat-stroke. Horses died of trypanosomiasis so that the Europeans, as well as their luggage, were sometimes carried on the heads of the local population. Probably a political officer in Sierra Leone (about 1890).

◁98. Mrs Powis, wife of a gold prospector, in camp in the Gold Coast (about 1910). The tin bath (left foreground) was a normal item of camp equipment but made a punishingly heavy load when packed full. Other familiar accessories are the Worcester sauce bottle on the folding camp-table and the Sparklet syphon on the ground. The Powis' wisely made themselves as comfortable as possible in bush, with basket chairs (probably bought at Madeira on the voyage out) and a pet bird in a cage, thoughtfully shaded by a sun hat. All this paraphernalia would have been brought in on the heads of carriers, or perhaps by canoe, as the camp appears to be on a river bank.

△99. Travelling with carriers: a surveyor in the high forest country of Sierra Leone (late 1930s). To carry a European's loads, including tent, bed, bath, kitchen, etc., required a gang of about twelve to fifteen carriers. It was sometimes necessary to take one or two extra to carry the food for the rest of the gang, and it is said that the carriers of the Congo explorer H.M. Stanley used to sing: 'We are the carriers who carry the loads of the carriers who carry the loads of the carriers [ad lib] who carry the loads of Mr Stanley.'

◁100. Carriers erecting a tent for a botanist from Kew who paid a scientific visit to the Cameroon highlands (about 1950). The high grasslands of Cameroon, running up to the 13,000-foot peak of Mount Cameroon, were the only part of West Africa to compare ecologically or scenically with the highlands of East Africa.

◁101. To the north of the areas of tse-tse infestation it was sometimes possible to hire pack animals, such as these camels being used by prospectors in Northern Nigeria (about 1910). Until the railway reached Kano in 1911, the trans-Saharan caravan trade still flourished.

△102. At the other end of the country: a trading agent and his African clerk arrive by canoe at a village landing-place in the delta creeks; their concern is probably with timber or palm oil. A deck chair set up in a small ('one puncheon') canoe, with a crew of half a dozen strong pullers, is a comparatively swift and comfortable means of transport. A palm-leaf roof against sun and rain would have added to the passengers' comfort.

103. Africa's main attraction for young men was probably the prospect it offered of a life of adventure, though they often ended up on an office stool. Yet sometimes a sporting bank manager such as Guy Betts of the British Bank of West Africa managed to take a weekend off to bag a bush cow near Zungeru (1937) or even an elephant, with sixty pounds of ivory a side, near Lake Chad.

104. Twenty years earlier, when the Chief Conservator of Forests, H.N. 'Timber' Thomson, went shooting on the Nigeria–Dahomey border there was still some really big ivory about.

105. Even the Chief Secretary to the Nigerian Government, J.A. Maybin, could sometimes escape from the Lagos secretariat to go fishing, and land this champion tarpon (1936).

◁106. A hammock bridge over the Tebenko River, Sierra Leone (1937). It is surprising how widely spread throughout the world is this ingenious type of do-it-yourself suspension bridge. In West Africa the material used was called 'tie-tie', a general pidgin term applying to any form of string or rope. For heavy-duty work such as this, the tie-tie would be from the stem of the calamus palm.

△107. With a cheerful and resourceful staff of 'boys' to carry the water, collect the firewood and cook the dinner on a stove made out of kerosene tins, we did not miss the amenities of civilization. These were the 'small boys' who did all the work. The District Officer's boundary settlement camp on the Ubiaja–Asaba border, Nigeria (late 1930).

13

═══ CULTURE CONTACT ═══

The colonialists may have seized power by force of arms, but cultural domination was often achieved with the co-operation of the colonized. The products of European culture were eagerly accepted in Africa: cloth, hardware, gin, firearms, in exchange for gold, ivory, slaves or whatever was required. But even before the export of slaves had ceased, the missionaries were also offering Christian teaching and education.

Such education was soon in great demand, since it also qualified for well-paid employment in government and commercial offices, and eventually produced the educated élites and politicians who were to demand self-government and freedom from colonial rule.

In the early colonial period, the Christian missions were the main channel through which Western education was introduced to the Africans, though mission schools were supervised and supported by grants from government. Regard for local religious susceptibilities and the wishes of the emirs resulted in both Christian missions and gin imports being confined to the non-Muslim areas, and it became necessary to introduce literate clerks and technicians of all kinds from the south to staff the commercial, administrative and technical installations in the Muslim north. At the same time, the administrative hierarchy established by the Fulani emirs so impressed Lugard that he was prepared to take it over almost as it stood, and it became the foundation of his celebrated system of indirect rule which was applied with varying success in the administration of British protectorates elsewhere in Africa.

The British found much to admire in the Islamic culture which they encountered in West Africa, and those who worked in the Nigerian emirates tended to adopt the Muslim attitude of disdain for the 'pagan' or mission-educated Southerners, whom the Fulani had regarded as slaves for the catching. Indeed, at one time, this attitude seems to have extended to include also their fellow Europeans who worked in Southern

Nigeria. It used to be said that only the necessity of keeping up appearances in front of the natives prevented the British of Northern Nigeria from declaring war on those of the South.

The Hausa language is widely spoken throughout Northern Nigeria and parts of the Sudan. It is not a difficult language for Europeans to learn and was generally spoken by those working in the area. Government officers all had to pass an examination in a local language before they could be confirmed in their appointment, but few attained much proficiency in any language except Hausa. The other languages were not widely spoken in a standard form and, being tonal, were difficult for Europeans to learn.

In 1849 Mrs Elizabeth Melville wrote from Sierra Leone:

I remember my wise reflection on hearing a European lady talk 'country fashion' to a black servant one day very shortly after my arrival, and my mental resolve that I would never profane my mother tongue by adopting so extraordinary a mode of speech... But necessity has gradually taught me to think differently, and I now give my household orders with perfect fluency, in a patois that would certainly puzzle both a linguist and a grammarian.[21]

Pidgin English spontaneously evolved as a common language between Africans and as useful means of communication. It consists mainly of a more or less garbled English vocabulary, with a few borrowings from other languages, and a simplified grammar which follows African constructions and usages. It has some attractive features, particularly the apt and humorous manipulation of English words to produce a sort of false derivation: as in 'breakfast' which becomes 'belly first' and 'detective' which becomes 'take t'ief'.

The one cultural sphere in which Europe seems to be prepared to learn from Africa is that of fine art. The Cubist and Post-Impressionist painters of the early years of the century found inspiration in the carvings of West Africa and the Congo. It took a generation or more for such appreciation to be generally accepted, but by the 1950s, a vogue for African art set the sale-room prices rocketing and dealers and their agents ransacking the sacred shrines of Africa.

Thanks to Kenneth Murray, an education officer of the old colonial government, legislation was passed to prohibit the export of Nigerian antiquities and much of the country's finest art is now preserved in its own museums. But the great collection of brass castings, taken from Benin by the Punitive Expedition of 1897, is still scattered through the museums and art collections of the world, and Nigeria has been obliged to buy it back at today's inflated prices.

108. A Koran school at Iseyin (about 1938). Such schools were in existence in Muslim Africa long before colonial times. Here the children learnt to repeat passages from the Koran by rote, which was possibly of little help in fitting them for life in a world which was unquestionably directed towards the West.

109. A local authority primary school in the Igbirra country (1937). Muslim dress is worn and instruction is in Hausa, but the area was not dominated by one of the powerful emirates, and Western-style education was encouraged with the aid of local-government funds.

◁110. Foundation Day celebrations at Ibadan University (1949). Four members of staff are followed by three students and a distinguished visitor from the North. At this stage, the University consisted of a collection of ex-Army huts, standing among the palms in old farmland outside Ibadan.

△111. An anatomy class at Yaba College Medical School (about 1949). As early as 1827 a college for the training of Anglican clergy was opened at Fourah Bay, Sierra Leone, but it was more than a hundred years before any other form of higher education became available (at Yaba College, Nigeria, or Achimota, Ghana). At Yaba, students could qualify as assistant medical officers for service in West Africa, but full medical training did not become available until the opening of Ibadan University.

◁ 112. A system of apprenticeship and special training schools produced skilled technicians, such as this surveyor of the Kano local administration.

△ 113. Formal education tended to be literary and academic. Shakespearian productions were a normal feature of the curriculum in secondary schools, with Gilbert and Sullivan as light relief. The natural dramatic talent of the actors triumphed over the difficulties presented by Elizabethan English and Victorian humour.
'Oh how I love thee. How I dote on thee': a unisex production by Ibadan Teachers' Training College (about 1950).

114. The Premier of Northern Nigeria and his Minister of Education inspect Capital School, Kaduna, where Cressida Bell, the Governor's daughter, is one of the pupils (1958).

115. Sales promotion for such a popular commodity as education took various forms.
Posters advertising the diversity of products handled by the United Africa
Company.

116. A small-scale scholastic supplier advertises some of his most popular titles in a Lagos backstreet.

117. Familiar advertisements appeared in local journals, adapted for the African student

118. and the general public.

119. A Nigerian infantry company and their British officers on the march. Another form of education was provided by the West African Frontier Force. West African troops served with distinction in the Second World War in the highlands of Ethiopia and the jungles of Burma. They returned home, having helped to free an African country from Italian rule and having seen the beginning of the end of the British raj in India. At the approach of independence, as in other departments of government, European officers were phased out. Since independence, both Ghana and Nigeria have been under military rule more often than not.

14

════════ HOME FROM HOME ════════

Some home amenities came remarkably early to the main administrative centres. Lagos had a race course by 1860 and was lit by electricity before the end of the century, while the sumptuous ritual hospitality of the viceregal garden-party was always an essential feature of the colonial scene.

The coming of motor-roads and furnished rest houses speeded up travel and added to the comfort of those whose aim was to get round the country as quickly as possible. Though I remember an occasion at the end of one financial year, when the motor transport vote was exhausted but the carrier vote was not, and my superior officer (with undue regard for Standing Orders) insisted that I should make a three-day trek through the bush with carriers which could have been completed in two hours by road.

Head offices expanded and paperwork proliferated, and even doctors and foresters spent more time in the office than in the hospital or the forest. As seniority overtook them, many found themselves inhabiting a tropical suburbia, spending their days behind an office desk and their evenings playing golf, snooker and bridge. Here, of course, they enjoyed the comforts of a sound roof, running water and electricity, and no one will undervalue these benefits who has spent the rainy season in a tent or under a leaky thatch, or tried to read by the fitful light of a kerosene lamp bombarded by flying insects, or bathed in six inches of muddy water.

Anomalous situations could arise when such amenities had been only partly installed. A new house might be provided with a flushing water-closet before a piped water supply was available. The house water tank then had to be filled daily by a line of labourers, head-loading buckets from a spring, which was hardly economic when compared with the removal of a single bucket from the old-style thunder-box.

Before refrigeration became general, the only readily obtainable fresh protein was in the form of the ubiquitous chicken and its eggs: to be bought in every market and the inevitable – and welcome – 'dash' from the local chief wherever you might spend the night. Variations on such a diet were sometimes available locally: sea or river fish or 'bush meat', usually some species of antelope. Normally, fishermen and hunters smoked their catch as soon as it was killed, and to shoot or fish for yourself was not a practicable means of regular supply.

Slaughter of domestic beef depended on local demand: a large, prosperous town would kill every day; a smaller one only one beast a week and the animals had often walked hundreds of miles before slaughter. In fact, the Frigidaire working off kerosene brought the luxury of cold-store meat and cold beer at a fairly early date to the man in the bush, as long as he was not too far in.

Eventually government found that it must be able to offer recruits the prospect of some sort of family life by the more generous provision of free passages for wives and children, and by the end of the colonial era, some home life in the white man's grave was at last possible.

The ultimate amenity which insulated the expatriate almost completely from Africa was air-conditioning. Today, I suppose, a European in Lagos or Takoradi can look out of the window of his air-conditioned office on to a scene of tower blocks and traffic jams and wonder whether he is in Tokyo or Manhattan.

120. Tea on the veranda in the house of a young Gold Coast government official (1910). The touch of a woman's hand is evident.

121. A more formal occasion at Government House, Freetown (1911). On the right is
a group of chiefs from the protectorate, and in the background to the left are
prominent citizens of the colony. We do not know the reason for the party, but it is
an occasion for swords and picture hats. On tower hill at the back is the Military
Hospital; of sinister size, it was probably intended to serve all the West Coast
territories.

122. A view from the back of Government House, Lagos (late 1940s). The British have created a remarkably faithful simulacrum of the English village: the big house overlooks the race course, an enlarged village green, on which a cricket match (Nigeria *v.* the Gold Coast) is in progress. In the foreground stands the Colonial Church, large enough to contain the European congregation who worshipped here with the Governor on Sundays. Examination of the car park will confirm the date.

123. 'Office work for District Commissioner Kpandu, and others like him, was always
sufficiently varied, especially so in 1942. He is addressing a meeting of Gold Coast
chiefs on the progress of the war, probably taking his cue from the poster on the
wall. The surrounding French colonial governments had declared for Vichy, but
luckily could not afford to give it much active support since Vichy racialism made
the régime most unpopular amongst the African population, The chiefs appear
content to leave matters in the hands of the District Commissioner.'

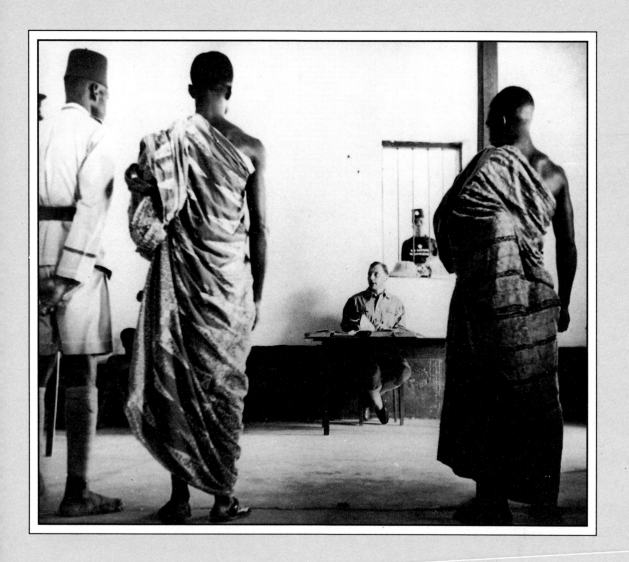

124. In his capacity as magistrate, D C Kpandu is hearing a smuggling case. Kpandu was in the old German colony of Togo, which, at the time, was administered as part of the Gold Coast under mandate from the League of Nations. In many small stations the D C (District Officer in Nigeria), as well as being the representative of the British Government and a magistrate, was also in charge of the police, prisons and indeed any other departments of government not represented by a departmental officer.

△ 125. Polo at Kaduna, Nigeria. Al Haji Kabira scores Kano's winning goal. It was possible to keep horses in the naturally tse-tse free environment of Northern Nigeria and also in the artificial conditions of some of the large Southern towns such as Lagos and Ibadan.

▷ 126. The Resident Bornu (Northern Nigeria) returning from a guinea-fowl shoot with a member of the Bornu District Council. Bird shooting – guinea-fowl, bush-fowl and duck – was a popular recreation which also helped to vary what could be a monotonous diet.

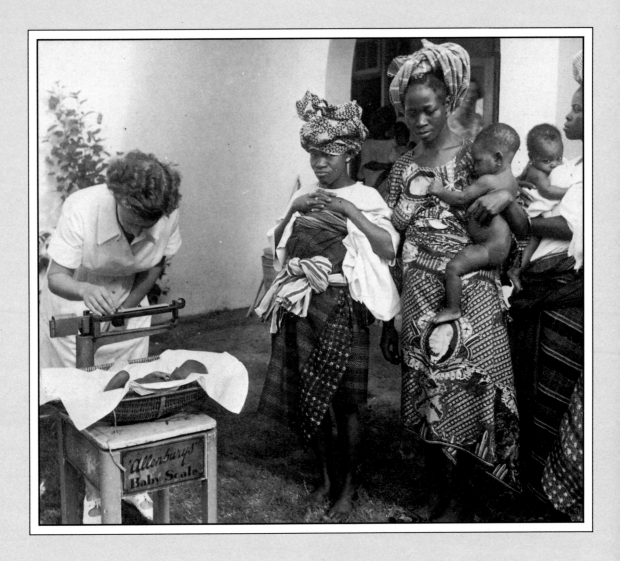

127. Many wives, with a rather more than adequate staff of servants, found
housekeeping was not a full-time job and took up voluntary work, such as this
mother-and-baby clinic in Yoruba country during the Second World War. The
woman on the right is wearing a patriotic print featuring firearms, aeroplanes and a
portrait of Churchill.

128. The District Officer of Okitipupa (a lonely station in the creeks of the Niger Delta) took a spare-time interest in the local football club.

◁129. A lecturer at Ibadan University, Brian Hopkins, enjoys one of the minor luxuries of life in Africa and has his hair cut at home by an itinerant barber. The pet lion cub in the foreground must have originated more than a hundred miles to the north of the Ibadan campus.

△130. Miss Katherine Margaret Bandele Omolere Adetoro Modupe Atkinson, and friends. At one time, the appearance of a white child in public attracted crowds like a circus parade, but after the Second World War, as local amenities improved and free passages for families were granted more generously, such sights became more common. When the daughter of a popular District Officer was born in the country, the local chiefs claimed the right to provide her with four Yoruba names in addition to her two English ones. *Bandele* means 'come home with me', and her father thinks that this may have been a sly reference to the approach of independence, when government officials and their families would be going home for the last time.

⊲131. Little Robert Marshall with his bucket and spade and his nanny, at the Lagos
seaside from which slaves in their thousands were being shipped across the Atlantic,
less than a hundred years before.

△132. Lagos from the top of the Shell building (1985): anonymously metropolitan.

15

════════ INDEPENDENCE ════════

After the last war, the bastions of colonialism fell one after another; or perhaps one could say, with equal truth, that the colonial powers laid down their burdens of responsibility, if not gladly, at least with resignation. When the word 'go' was given by Ghana in 1957, there was almost as much of a scramble to get out of Africa as there had been to get in seventy years before. Ten years later, we had all gone: British, French, Belgians. Only the Portuguese hung on: first to come and last to go, like awkward guests at a drinks party.

The sudden acquisition of African colonies by European powers in the late nineteenth century and the equally sudden relinquishment of those colonies only seventy years later is difficult to explain in isolation, influenced as it was by larger political forces around the world. At the end of the last century, imperial appendages were seen as adding to the wealth and glory of the European nation state, and Africa was the only area in which they could be acquired without risking conflict with some other great power. Fifty years later, the possession of colonies hardly seemed justifiable morally or even economically.

As early as 1920, the National Congress of British West Africa, representing the views of the élites of Lagos, Accra and Freetown, had proposed the constitution of a self-governing Dominion of British West Africa. But this form of political development was not encouraged by the British and the political parties which emerged at the end of the Second World War aimed at full national independence. The United Nations Charter had asserted the right of all people to choose their own form of government, and the British had shown in India that they really were prepared to consider the dismemberment of the Empire.

From 1945 onwards, in an attempt to ease the transition to independence, the adoption of a new constitution had been an almost annual event in one or other of the British West African territories. Such frequent changes were most confusing, and the reasons for them were not always apparent.

The newly appointed Nigerian Minister for Agriculture and National Resources complained to me that when he had been Chairman of the Idanre District Council, he had written to the Chief Conservator of Forests, requesting a reduction in the area of the Idanre Forest Reserve, to allow more land for farming; now, as Minister of Government, he was obliged to uphold official Forest Policy and refuse his own request.

Rival political parties, often with a tribal basis, delayed the final achievement of independence. The conservative and less-developed northern territories of Nigeria, the Gold Coast and Sierra Leone mistrusted the more sophisticated coastal people who had hitherto taken the lead politically, but no politician could afford to appear to be opposing self-government and freedom.

Ghana finally led the field in 1957, followed three years later by Nigeria, and in the same year thirteen ex-French territories in West and Central Africa became independent, as did the Congo. To the last, de Gaulle hoped to form a Franco-African community that would embrace all the former French colonial territories in Africa, but the lure of complete independence was too strong. Indeed, when Guinea became independent she concluded a short-lived union with Ghana.

Nigeria's freedom celebrations were extended over a period of nearly four years, partly on account of the reluctance of the Muslim North to agree to the form of constitution under which independence should be achieved. The process was completed in two stages. Internal self-government was granted to the western and eastern regions by the Queen in person and, two years later, to the North by the Duke of Gloucester. At the final national independence celebrations in 1960 the Crown was represented by Princess Alexandra. By the end of this long-drawn-out process, it is not surprising if the final jubilations were rather less than rapturous.

A few weeks after the final celebrations, I was talking to the old chief of a northern Yoruba village, and he asked me: 'Is it true that we are no longer ruled by white men?' I told him: 'Yes, you have got your freedom now.' He turned to the local man who was acting as my guide and said: 'How did you get a white man to stay with you? I should like one to stay with me.' We all laughed, because it was a sort of courteous joke, but it also expressed a fairly widespread apprehension at the prospect of complete freedom.

"My Dark Lady"
—or "The New Pygmalion"

◁133. The old colonialist makes way for the blandishments of the commercial carpet-baggers. But West Africa, at any rate, parted more graciously from her erstwhile protector than is suggested in this cartoon, published in the quarterly *Optima* in March 1962.

△134. The first meeting of the democratically elected Parliament of Ghana (1951). Kwame Nkrumah stands eighth from the right. He had been released from gaol when his party won the election. Those released with him proudly called themselves 'prison graduates'. Six years later, Nkrumah became the President of the first West African territory to achieve independence from colonial rule. The photographer has arranged his exposure to allow for the black faces, with the result that the white ones appear, symbolically, to be fading away.

◁135. A Queen's visit: the first and last. In 1957, East and West Nigeria achieved internal self-government, which was granted by the Queen in person. Among the Nigerian notables presented to Her Majesty was the Oba of Benin; he wears his traditional regalia composed of thousands of coral beads. His once powerful kingdom was first visited by Europeans at the end of the fifteenth century and gave its name to the Bight of Benin, of which we were warned to 'beware'.

△136. The last British Governor of Northern Nigeria, Sir Gawain Bell, on his first arrival in the country in 1957, is welcomed by the Emir of Kano. After only three years in the post, the Government of Northern Nigeria paid Sir Gawain the compliment of asking him to stay on during the first two years of independence.

137. Northern Nigeria was at first reluctant to accept independence, and the grant of self-government was postponed until 1959, when the Duke of Gloucester read the proclamation at the northern capital of Kaduna. (From left to right: the Duke and Duchess of Gloucester, the Shehu of Bornu, Sir James Robertson, the last white Governor-General of Nigeria, Lady Robertson and the Sardauna of Sokoto.) The Sardauna holds a programme of events entitled 'Durbar': a memento of another empire.

138. The Fulani emirates have a traditional flair for pageantry that was given full
play on this occasion. The Emir of Kano leading the parade on his camel is about
to eclipse Lady Robertson.

139. Harold Macmillan, then British Prime Minister, and the Sardauna of Sokoto, then Prime Minister of Northern Nigeria: a pair of astute politicians. Shortly before Nigerian independence, Macmillan visited Ghana and Nigeria on his way to Cape Town where, referring to the number of African states which were to become independent during the year, he announced: 'the wind of change is blowing through the continent'.

140. On the eve of independence, Nigeria bids farewell to the colonial power: Princess Alexandra and Nigerian schoolchildren on Lagos race course.

REFERENCES

Life in the White Man's Grave

1. R. Hakluyt, *Principal Navigations of the English Nation*, vol. IV, London, 1907, pp. 55–6 (originally published 1599).
2. R. Coupland, *The British Anti-Slavery Movement*, London, 1933, p. 59.
3. C. Howard (ed.), *West African Explorers*, Oxford, 1951, p. 77.
4. M. Park, *Travels*, London, 1907, pp. 100, 149.
5. Sir A. Burns, *History of Nigeria*, London, 1948, p. 139.
6. A. C. G. Hastings, *The Voyage of the 'Dayspring'*, London, 1926, p. 33.
7. W. B. Baikie, *Narrative of an Exploring Voyage up the Rivers Kwora and Benue*, London, 1856, p. 386.
8. M. Perham, *Lugard: The Years of Authority*, London, 1960, p. 14.
9. Colonial Secretariat, Lagos, circular of 29 December 1893.
10. Sir W. MacGregor, *Touring Notes*, June 1900.
11. M. Perham, *Lugard: The Years of Authority*, p. 446.
12. M. J. Echeruo, *Victorian Lagos*, London, 1977, p. 1.
13. M. Perham, *Lugard: The Years of Authority*, pp. 597, 466.
14. Sir A. Burns, *History of Nigeria*, p. 139.
15. R. Lander, *Captain Clapperton's Last Expedition to Africa*, vol. II, London, 1830, p. 154.
16. R. Kipling, 'The New Knighthood', London, 1927.
17. K. Post, *The New States of West Africa*, London, 1964, pp. 18, 19.

The Pictures

1. R. Hakluyt, *Principal Navigations of the English Nation*, vol. IV, pp. 43–4.
2. ibid., vol. III, pp. 5, 13.
3. N. Owen, *Journal of a Slave Dealer*, London, 1930, p. 91.
4. W. Bosman, *Description of the Coast of Guinea*, London, 1907, pp. 49–50, 107–8.
5. W. Reade, *The African Sketch Book*, vol. III, London, 1873, pp. 178–9.
6. W. G. Hynes, *The Economics of Empire*, London, 1979, p. 44.
7. W. Reade, *Savage Africa*, London, 1864, p. 406.
8. R. Burton, *Wanderings in West Africa*, vol. II, London, 1863, p. 166.

9. ibid., vol. I, p. 217.
10. J. Grace, *Domestic Slavery in West Africa*, London, 1975, p. 251.
11. Glover to the Duke of Newcastle, 6 November 1863.
12. A. H. M. Kirk-Greene, 'A Preliminary Note on New Resources for Nigerian Military History', *Journal of the Historical Society of Nigeria*, vol. III, no. 1, 1964
13. M. Perham, *Lugard: The Years of Authority*, p. 17.
14. ibid., p. 24.
15. Sir A. Burns, *History of Nigeria*, p. 170.
16. M. Perham, *Lugard: The Years of Authority*, p. 90.
17. D. Porch, *The Conquest of the Sahara*, London, 1985, p. 127.
18. M. Perham, *Lugard: The Years of Authority*, p. 550.
19. D. Livingstone, *Last Journals*, vol. I, London, 1874, p. 13.
20. R. Jobson, *The Golden Trade*, Teignmouth [1904], pp. 190–91.
21. E. Melville, *A Residence in Sierra Leone*, London, 1849, p. 3.

SELECT BIBLIOGRAPHY

Baikie, W. B., *Narrative of an Exploring Voyage up the Rivers Kwora and Benue* (London, 1856)

Barth, H., *Travels and Discoveries in North and Central Africa* (London, 1858)

Bosman, W., *Description of the Coast of Guinea* (London, 1907)

Burns, Sir A., *History of Nigeria* (London, 1948)

Burton, R., *Wanderings in West Africa*, 2 vols. (London, 1863)

— *Abeokuta and the Cameroons Mountain* (London, 1863)

Cole, W., *Life in the Niger* (London, 1862)

Coupland, R., *The British Anti-Slavery Movement* (London, 1933)

Crowther, Rev. S., *Journal of an Expedition up the Niger and Tshadda Rivers* (London, 1855)

Crozier, F. P., *Five Years Hard* (London, 1932)

Echeruo, M. J., *Victorian Lagos* (London, 1977)

Fage, J. D., *Introduction to the History of West Africa* (Cambridge, 1955)

— *Ghana* (London, 1961)

Fyfe, C., *Sierra Leone: A Short History* (London, 1979)

Grace, J., *Domestic Slavery in West Africa* (London, 1975)

Hakluyt, R., *The Principal Navigations of the English Nation*, 8 vols. (London, 1907)

Hastings, A. C. G., *The Voyage of the 'Dayspring'* (London, 1926)

Hatch, J., *Nigeria* (London, 1971)

Heneker, W. C., *Bush Warfare* (London, 1907)

Howard, C. (ed.), *The West African Explorers* (Oxford, 1951)

Hynes, W. G., *The Economics of Empire* (London, 1979)

Jobson, R., *The Golden Trade* (Teignmouth, [1904])

Johnson, S., *The History of the Yorubas* (Lagos, 1937)

Johnston, H. H., *The Negro in the New World* (London, 1910)

Kingsley, M., *Travels in West Africa* (London, 1897)

— *West African Studies* (London, 1901)

Laird, M. and Oldfield, R. A., *Narrative of an Expedition into the Interior of Africa*, 2 vols. (London, 1837)

Lander, R., *Captain Clapperton's Last Expedition to Africa*, 2 vols. (London, 1830)

Lander, R. and Lander, J., *Journal of an Expedition to Explore the Course and Termination of the Niger*, 3 vols. (London, 1833)

Lloyd, A., *The Drums of Kumasi* (London, 1964)

Melville E., *A Residence in Sierra Leone* (London, 1849)

'Nemo' [A. C. Douglas], *Niger Memories* (Exeter, 1937)

Newton, J., *The Journal of a Slave Trader* (London, 1962)

Owen, N., *Journal of a Slave Dealer* (London, 1930)

Park, M., *Travels* (London, 1907)

Perham, M., *Lugard: The Years of Adventure* (London, 1960)

— *Lugard: The Years of Authority* (London, 1960)

— *The Diaries of Lord Lugard*, 4 vols. (London, vols. I–III, 1959; vol. IV, 1963)

Porch, D., *The Conquest of the Sahara* (London, 1985)

Post, K., *The New States of West Africa* (London, 1964)

Reade, W., *Savage Africa* (London, 1864)

— *The African Sketch Book*, 2 vols. (London, 1873)

Smith, R. S., *The Lagos Consulate* (London, 1978)

Vandeleur, S., *Campaigning on the Upper Niger and Nile* (London, 1898)

Whitford, J., *Trading Life in Western and Central Africa* (Liverpool, 1877)

INDEX

Figures in bold type indicate page numbers of illustrations